GET THE GIRL

GET THE GIRL

HOW TO BE THE KIND OF MAN
THE KIND OF WOMAN YOU WANT TO MARRY
WOULD WANT TO MARRY

DOUGLAS WILSON

CANON PRESS

MOSCOW, IDAHO

Published by Canon Press
P. O. Box 8729, Moscow, Idaho 83843
800-488-2034 | www.canonpress.com

Douglas Wilson, *Get the Right Girl: Be the Kind of Man the Kind of Woman You Want to Marry Would Want to Marry*
Copyright ©2022 by Douglas Wilson

Unless otherwise noted, all Scripture quotations are from the King James Version.

Scripture quotations marked...
* ESV are from the Holy Bible, English Standard Version. Copyright © 2001 by Crossway, a publishing ministry of Good News Publishers. Used by permission.
* NIV are from the Holy Bible, New International Version®, NIV®. Copyright © 1973, 1978, 1984, 2011 by Biblica, Inc.™ Used by permission.
* NKJV are from the New King James Version®. Copyright ©1982 by Thomas Nelson, Inc. Used by permission.
* NASB 2020 are from the New American Standard Bible 2020, Copyright © 1960, 1971, 1977, 1995, 2020 by The Lockman Foundation. Used by permission.

22 23 24 25 26 27 28   10 9 8 7 6 5 4 3

Dedication:
To all my real nephews—
Davis, Dane, Graham, Gunn, Masis, Scott, and Luke—
who all got married without this book being in print yet.

CONTENTS

FOREWORD

Life between the sexes has always been good for generating pastoral challenges, but we live in a generation that has figured out how to multiply, compound, and complicate such challenges.

A number of New Testament epistles devote some significant column inches to instructing husbands and wives on how to get along. Because of the differences between men and women, and because of the disposition to selfishness that was introduced to all of us by the Fall, you would think that this would be enough to keep us busy.

And so it was, but then we introduced a host of other complications—including, but not limited to, an inability to define *man* or *woman*, the widespread availability of contraception, the widespread availability of pornography, the entrance of women en masse into the work force, the cultural shifts that resulted when the average age for marriage was delayed by many years, the widespread acceptance of feminist assumptions, and so on.

Although Christians are not enthusiastic participants in many of these shifts, they are nonetheless still *affected* by them.

In the old days, back before all this, the standards were at least clear. The difficulty was that because of our sinful fallenness, we had trouble meeting the standards that both we and our surrounding culture acknowledged. But because of our theological laziness and indolence, we have now allowed the rot of sin to get into the standards themselves. It used to be that everyone recognized that it was a rotten move to impregnate a woman and then leave her. But now? She should have been on the pill. What do you expect? A *generous* move would be for the father to offer to pay for half the cost of the abortion. And so on.

Christians are dismayed by this kind of thing, particularly when it gets to issues like abortion or same sex immorality. But even though Christians are dismayed by it, as stated earlier, they are still affected by these shifts. When non-Christians marry later and later, it turns out that Christians are following the same demographic shifts—either because they are copying the non-Christians or, as is more likely, they are all responding to the same cultural pressures.

And when it comes to things like homosexual behavior, because we are conservative Christians, we register our "disagreement." But our great-grandfathers would have been outraged and appalled, and they probably would also have been appalled with our mild "disagreement."

Because of all this, when it comes to issues like dating, courtship, and marriage, it is important for Christians to learn how to be *intentionally* countercultural. If we have not decided, intentionally, to swim upstream, then we have almost certainly decided, unintentionally, to float downstream. And because most of us dozed off in our inner tubes, we are now bobbing around in the Gulf of Mexico, staring at the oil rigs, and trying to figure out what direction the coast might be. I speak in a parable.

For these reasons, and a few others, I decided to write a series of letters to an entirely fictional nephew. There is no Dawson. There are, however, many situations out there that mirror Dawson's plight almost exactly. These letters are for the men who must do something about them.

Douglas Wilson
April 2022

ONE

LIFE IN GIRL WORLD

Dear Dawson,

Thanks for contacting me. I actually wasn't that surprised to hear from you, but I was perhaps a little surprised at how much detail you were able to provide. You have clearly done your homework, and I am glad you are working through these issues. You are clearly taking things seriously.

Dealing with the breakup of a long term relationship is always hard, and this is particularly the case when you didn't see it coming. You were shopping for a ring I gather, and she was apparently thinking that she could probably do better. That kind of thing is a punch in the gut, and there is no way around it.

Your questions are very good ones, and it is going to take me more than one letter to work through them. But I trust that you can put up with hearing from me from time to time—you have always been a most dutiful nephew.

So I want to work through this systematically. Think of this as a series of letters from an old guy on life between the sexes. Some of what I say will seem like it is straight out of the Bible, some of it will seem like it is commonsense obvious, and some of it will seem to you to be wildly inappropriate and possibly illegal.

Judging from some of the books and websites you mentioned, I think it would be good to begin there. Your initial attraction to them was understandable, certainly, but there is real bitterness there, and there are profound spiritual hazards in that kind of bitterness. And the "manosphere" online is filled with a certain kind of red-pilled bitterness which, when it is coupled with evolutionary and materialistic assumptions, produces an odd mix of appalling selfishness and cynicism (and reductionism with regard to sex) coupled with common grace insights that you would never hear from an evangelical beta-preacher. So as you read such stuff you need to take that phrase *caveat emptor*, soak it in lighter fluid, and set it on fire.

The first thing to fix in your mind would be the doctrine of creation and fall. God made the sexes different on purpose. The basic outline of those differences is a design feature, and not a flaw. It is not the result of evolutionary adaptions, groping blindly in the dark. That is the creational foundation. The second factor to consider is sin. That creational set of initial differences has been marred by sin. In men, it has been marred in one direction, and in women it has been marred in another. But suppose yourself married to a godly woman, that godliness will not erase her essential femininity. And suppose you are walking closely with the Lord—that will not erase your masculinity.

Think of it this way. God created the man and the woman in order that they together might sing a duet, each with their respective part. Let us say that he is singing at one pitch and she is harmonizing with another. That is the creational difference. And when music harmonizes well, there are few things more glorious.

Enter sin. This means that he is now singing his part flat and she is singing her part sharp. When that starts happening, it sounds like nothing on earth. Nothing is worse than a sinful man and a sinful woman trying to get along. We tend to think that the problem is that they are singing something different (which is what harmony is), when the problem is that they are singing something different poorly. When you couple that with the fact that you are singing flat yourself, and playing the role of music critic at the same time, the predictable result is quarrels and gross misunderstandings.

So one of the solutions that people come up with is the makeshift solution of trying to sing in unison. They don't know how to be distinctively masculine or distinctively feminine while staying on pitch, and so they pick one part, and insist that both sing that part.

In masculinist societies, that part has been the male one, and the women are required to just go along. In a feminist society, such as ours now is, it is the reverse. The basic framework of expectations is the feminine one, and the men are required to just go along. This is what I call life in girl world.

Everything is quite a jumble, and there are more than a few aspects of it that have everybody confused. Here is an illustration—the ubiquity of porn. This is a really serious problem, but the worst thing about the problem is that nobody appears to understand what the problem actually is. It is described for us as an example of the "male gaze," or "toxic masculinity," or the "objectification of women." There are problems with all of that, of course, but what porn actually does is take male sexuality and hook it up to a heavy morphine drip.

A generation ago, when I got married, the average age for marriage was twenty-two—right out of college. Now the average age, for men and women both, is in the late twenties. This is not because young men are refusing to get off the dime for some mysterious reason. Rather, this is a structural, systemic, societal problem, one that we have all together created for ourselves, and the borders of which we rigorously police.

I will finish with this observation. Your letter indicated that you thought a big part of the problem with your ex-girlfriend is that she had been "affected by feminism." What I would like you to meditate on is something that goes in what you might think is a surprising direction. I think that it is just as likely that the breakup was because you have been affected by feminism.

Again, this is what I mean by life in girl world. The women have been affected by it, of course, but so have the men. Men are expected to behave in a certain way, and so are the women, but women have proven less adaptable to the dictates of this anti-creational nonsense. In other words, both sexes will repeat their egalitarian catechism answers, but the women continue to do what women have always wanted to do, which is to marry up. Women are hypergamous, and they continue to make their decisions on this basis, despite the egalitarian rhetoric.

Men have made more of an effort to fit in with the new egalitarian imperative, and then are surprised at the fact that the women don't respond romantically to what the women appear to be demanding rhetorically. Right? You mentioned the guy that your ex is now dating, and the fact that he is in fact what she falsely accused you of being. You described him as being something of an alpha jerk, and she went for him after saying that you weren't sensitive enough. What kind of sense does that make?

But it makes all the sense in the world, if you look at the world the way God made it, and stop listening to the lies that we tell ourselves about the brave, new world we are supposedly constructing. We are doing no such thing. We are just simply growing increasingly befuddled about the old world—the one God ordained for us to live in. Because like it or not, that is the world we live in.

We must look at what God's Word says, first, and then secondly look at how the world actually functions. Stop listening to what all the pundits and experts say, and look at what women do. Then look at what men do. And then take that to the Word.

Your uncle,
Douglas

TWO

EVOLUTION AND SEXUAL SELFISHNESS

Dear Dawson,

Thanks for your quick reply. I gather this entire subject has your interest.

So I want to start by picking up on one of the central ramifications of something I mentioned to you in my first letter. It is really important that you banish every form of evolutionary thought from your calculations. The sexual differences between men and women are created, and they were then bent by the fall. They are not the result of evolutionary "strategies," with women developing their own set of them, and men developing theirs. The relationship between the sexes is not the result of blind groping at the cellular level, but rather purposive and intentional, a gift from God.

In the former, we have a haphazard arrangement that men and women have to negotiate with their own peculiar sexual goals in mind. In the latter we have an intricate organism, meticulously designed by God, one which is accompanied by a user's manual. And there is a vast difference between life in that first world and life in the second. More about that in a minute.

God created man in His own image, male and female. "So God created man in his own image, in the image of God created he him; male and female created he them" (Gen. 1:27, ESV). And in the verse immediately prior to this, He established the cultural mandate for all of humanity, expecting them to exercise dominion over the earth and all of its creatures.

I know you are familiar with the whole concept of intelligent design when it comes to certain mechanisms like the falcon's eye, or an eagle's feather, or how the liver functions, or a monkey's tail, or any number of other "irreducibly complex" interactions. The complexity of all these things is beyond staggering, and yet the relationship of a man and a woman puts all of them in the shade: "There be three things which are too wonderful for me, Yea, four which I know not: The way of an eagle in the air; The way of a serpent upon a rock; The way of a ship in the midst of the sea; And the way of a man with a maid" (Prov. 30:18–19).

The doctrine of creation means that the relationship of a man and a woman is beyond marvelous. But sin has made the relationship between them discordant. The redemption offered through Christ sets them back on the path again, albeit with more than a few bumps along the way. Those bumps are the result of the man learning to overcome his sinful tendencies and the woman learning to overcome hers.

Picture a guitar badly out of tune, and then try to picture accounting for this in two different ways— by the way of evolution or the way of creation and fall. If you thought the guitar evolved randomly, you would not be inclined to complain about how out of tune it is, but rather would be amazed that it could make any sound at all. Imagine all those pieces of wood coming together in complete darkness, and the metal for the keys mining itself, and the spacing of the frets, and winding of the strings, all sharing a total absence of any intentionality. That is the idea of evolution. There is no overall telos.

Now imagine a master craftsman making a beautiful guitar, with each piece exquisitely formed and placed, and then after it is placed on its rack it is left alone for a month, and it goes out of tune. That is creation and fall.

When a representative of each school of thought explains why the instrument sounds so bad, their explanations will be completely different. One will say that further evolution is needed, and the other will say that the guitar needs to be tuned, in order to be brought into conformity with its obvious purpose.

Not only will the explanations be different, so also will the practical strategies of the men and women involved be different. Over time, people will act in a manner consistent with their basic worldview. If all that matters are the dictates of the selfish gene, then logic says that a male will want to impregnate as many females as he can, so that his numerous progeny might have a greater chance of survival, and the female will want to attract the attentions of an alpha male so that her offspring will have a greater chance of survival. And let the sex games begin.

By way of contrast, when a man and a woman have submitted themselves to God and His Word and entered a monogamous relationship, bound by covenant, in the light of His Word, their stations are assigned to them. The one who assigns them is the one who designed the whole thing in the first place. We don't have to figure it out ourselves, following the instructions of our own selfish and very sinful proclivities. But when we submit ourselves to Him and obey Him, we are tuning the instrument, not inventing the instrument.

Let me make another musical illustration, but this time in the context of one man and one woman. Say we want them to sing a duet, in harmony. Let us say that the piece as composed really is beautiful, and that the harmonization as written is wonderful and glorious. As they sing together, the man and the woman are singing completely different parts. While he is singing a G, for example, she is singing a C. When voices blend like this, the way they are supposed to, and the harmony is tight, there are few things on this earth more beautiful.

But now suppose we can still recognize the part that each was supposed to be singing, but we hear that he is just sludging along with it, singing pretty flat. And she for her part, trying to compensate in a weird way, is singing sharp. In this scenario, the sound is like nothing on earth, and not in a good way.

Masculinity and femininity were created by God to harmonize, not compete, and when a man and a woman are walking with God, they do harmonize. "But if we walk in the light, as he is in the light, we have fellowship one with another, and the blood of Jesus Christ his Son cleanseth us from all sin" (1 John 1:7).

There is no way for a man and a woman to be in fellowship with God and not to be in fellowship with each other. In the world, on evolutionary assumptions, it is possible for a man and a woman to come to some sort of negotiated settlement, but when that happens one of them will have won and one of them will have lost. Somebody got the better end of the deal.

It is easier to sing unison than to sing in harmony, so in some marriages the man browbeats the woman so that she loses her distinctive feminine voice and is required to sing his part along with him. In other homes, which is far more common these days, the man is the one who is required to abandon his distinctive masculine voice—the woman carries the melody, and he hums in the background like a servant leader.

Within a secular framework, egalitarians and feminists want the women to win, and within that same framework, the reactionary men's movement want the men to win. The result, predictably, is strife—ongoing strife. And as they carry on their love/hate thing, believing Christians can observe from the side. As we do, we will find that the women can and do say lots of pointed and insightful things about the men, and the men can do the same in return. But despite whatever points are scored, there is no real hope for any harmony.

Men and women are so different, and the world is so broken and fallen, that there is no way for us to get along unless these sexual games have authoritative umpires all over the field, not to mention authoritative coaches all along the men's bench, and all along the women's bench. Without those umpires and coaches, the players are sent out onto a big open field, their bodies full of hormones, to play a game that has no rules, no boundaries, and no overarching point. The result is the chaos that we now see.

In case my analogy was unclear, the umpires and coaches are the standards and assigned sex roles given to men and women in the Scriptures. If the Scriptures tell the man to be the pitcher, he doesn't get to go out to left field. If the woman is told to play in left field, she must come out of left field (in one sense) in order to take her place in left field. Scriptures assign our positions (coaches) and Scriptures tell us the rules of play (umpires).

But in God's economy, the relationship between a man and a women, bound together in covenant, is a relationship that is truly sensible, full of good sense. God created us to function as one flesh. This means that a godly man and godly woman are one instrument with two parts, like a violin and a bow, or one mechanism with two parts, like a lock and a key—or like one flesh, with a man and a woman.

As you have questions, please send them on, but in my next letter I hope to cover how sexual all of this is. All of human life is sexual, top to bottom, front to back, side to side.

Your uncle,
Douglas

THREE

NOT THE SAME THING AT ALL

Dear Dawson,

I am glad that I appear to be getting at the crux of your questions. What I want to do in this letter is discuss equity and equality, and how we are to understand those words when it comes to life between the sexes.

Egalitarianism has been a true intellectual corruption, and it is the kind of corruption that has gotten into everything. It worked it way into our collective heart in the form of envy, and worked it way out in our collective mind in the form of what is called "equality." It has even crept (largely unnoticed) into the assumptions of many conservative believers. So we have to be careful working through this. There are layers.

Biblical equity means that that we are to apply the same standard to all, whether Jew or Greek, slave or free, male or female. At this first layer, we do this because we want to get the same equitable result. When someone is charged with a crime, for example, we require two or three witnesses for a conviction. We do this because if someone is charged with shoplifting, say, whether it is a man or a woman, we want the same rules applied and we want the same results as a consequence of applying those same rules. We want the guilty man (or woman) to be convicted, and we want the innocent man (or woman) to be acquitted. We want the same rules so that we can get the same results. We want equity in the application of the rules and we want equity in the results. That is the first layer, and it is pretty straightforward. That would be equity.

But the next layer is a bit different. Here we want the same rules for all, knowing that it will wind up with completely different results. This is equity also, but the result is inequality of result. But even though there is inequality of result, there is no inequity.

If we were to have a foot race, and we included men and women both, and we applied the same standards to all, the consequence would be that the men would win a disproportionate number of the races. This, even though they all had the same starting line, the same starting pistol, the same stop watch, and the same finish line. If you treat them all the same in this scenario, the results will be completely different. Inequality, but no inequity.

Because of the obvious physiological differences between men and women, up until ten minutes ago, we had men competing against men in their own divisions and women competing against women. This is why we (rightly) had men's sports and women's sports, and why the tranny thing is so screaming ridiculous. It is ridiculous because we are applying level one standards to a level two situation.

But the necessity-of-inequality principle still stands, even within those different divisions. Equality of opportunity here results in disparate outcomes—not everyone gets the gold medal. Only one woman wins that medal, and in his division, only one man. Not everyone establishes a world record. Not everyone runs the same speed. There is inequality in the outcome, but no inequity in the rules of the competition.

But please note. These will be different outcomes when you apply equitable rules to men and women, when those men and women are all doing the same thing, laboring to achieve the same goal—which is getting to the finish line first.

But sex is completely different. Men and women are both sexual beings, but their sexuality is completely different. A man and a woman running the 100-yard dash, running shoulder to shoulder, are doing the same thing differently. But when it comes to a man and a woman in an erotic relationship, face to face, they are doing completely different things. He is making love to a woman, and she is not. She is making love to a man, and he is not. They are both making love, but as individuals they are not doing the same thing at all.

And the difference is not to be found in the fact that they are giving one another pleasure, unlike a foot race. If they were to exchange foot rubs, or scratch an itch between one another's shoulder blades, they would be giving the same pleasure to one another because in those respects their bodies are very much alike. Sore feet are sore feet. But with regard to sex, their bodies are completely different.

So sex is therefore in a different category entirely. The same thing, a lovemaking session, is the result of two different people, with different bodies, with different desires, different motives, different emotions, and different purposes, doing very different things. He receives by giving, and she gives by receiving—and yet they both give and both receive. But differently.

I once wrote something on this topic that caused a great deal of outrage and consternation, but I will go ahead and say it again. It caused that outrage because egalitarianism is such a capricious goddess, and is very easily displeased. But sex is not an egalitarian pleasuring party. Sex is nothing like a foot rub.

And this is where the egalitarianism has crept into many of our assumptions, even among conservatives. We have been repeatedly told that women are as interested in sex as men are, and the problem is that this is almost completely false. Notice that I say almost. It is not as though he is playing chess, and she is in another room playing Scrabble. Of course in one sense they are doing the same thing, and both are interested in the same thing, but that is not what we really need to be reminded of. A woman can be as interested in sex as a man, but the nature of her interest is completely different.

We need to be reminded of how different it is for both because we have been subjected to unrelenting propaganda that stoutly maintains that apart from the minor concave/convex part, men and women approach sex in the same way. This is simply a lie. Furthermore it is the lie that undergirds the whole transsexual debacle. The undeniable physiological difference between men and women is, for dogmatic reasons, regarded as a detail, addressable via surgery, and all that is needed is for a person to decide what sex they are going to be, like deciding what you are going to major in at college. But it is nothing like that at all.

Now I know that I am describing a man and woman in a sexual relationship, which is not your situation right now. But you would certainly like it to be your situation, and what I am saying here is going to be relevant to how you might be enabled to get to that point, so please bear with me.

The interest that men have in sex and the interest that women have in sex are interests that bear very little resemblance to one another. It is true that we could say that the phrase "water flowing" is a descriptive phrase, but keep in mind that this could include a narrow waterfall crashing onto rocks a thousand feet below, and it would also apply to the Mississippi River, a mile wide, rolling on to the sea. In both cases, water is flowing but the differences are more obvious than the similarities.

A man's sexual cycle runs from arousal to climax. A woman's sexual cycle runs from arousal to when the kid graduates from college. He is the narrow waterfall, and she is the Mississippi. A man's sexual interest is very intense while it lasts, and very much on the surface. A woman's sexual interest is broad and deep. A man's sexual focus is largely limited to one part of his body and is almost incidental to him. A woman's sexual focus involves almost her whole body. And to come to the most crucial point, the sex act is an act of biological reproduction, and the woman is the one who gets pregnant.

This is the key to understanding everything, and it is why our current elites are so bent on persuading us—contrary to creation, reason, good order, common sense, and Holy Scripture—that men can get pregnant too. And all of this together means that while the man and the woman have a point of connection in "having had sex together," their experience of the whole thing remains very different. Their attitudes toward the whole enterprise are not the same. Moreover, they cannot be the same.

All this is another way of saying that when it comes to the experience of sex, men and women do not share the same worldview. Of course, if they are both Christians they can take a step back and share the same biblical worldview about sex, knowing what Scripture teaches about sex roles and so on. But with regard to the experience of sex, men don't understand women and women don't understand men. This is not a flaw in the design—it is a feature, not a bug. We are not supposed to understand each other.

The reason men and women feel so differently about it is because it is different. Remember what I said in the previous letter about this being designed. It is not a flaw. It is not a blind evolutionary adaptation. It is a creation feature, marred by sin, which we will get to in a minute.

Both men and women have testosterone in their bodies, and testosterone is a major factor when it comes to their libido, for men and women both. A woman's ovaries make testosterone and a man's testes make testosterone. So everything is the same, right? The difference is that an average man has about 15 to 20 times the amount of testosterone sloshing around in his body as an average woman does. This, um, has an impact on things, on

how the world appears to each of them. It means
that his outlook is very different from her outlook.

Okay, so how is all this relevant? And what difference does it make to you?

According to a cluster of old myths, the seer
Tiresias once displeased Hera, and was turned into
a woman for seven years as a consequence. Later
on he was struck blind by her because Zeus and
Hera were having an argument about whether men
or women enjoyed sex more. Since Tiresias had
been both a man and a woman, he was called upon
to settle the question. He said that "of ten parts man
enjoys one only." This was not the right answer according to Hera, and so she blinded him. Now this
story really doesn't illuminate anything, except to
underscore the fact that one half of the human race
has no conception of what it is like to be the other
half. There is a chasm of ignorance here.

And that chasm of ignorance is not bridged
when a man goes under the knife. He does not
now know what it is like to be a woman. Rather, he
knows what it is like to be a eunuch, and he also
knows what it is like to be flattered and lied to by
idiots, but he is not an inch closer to knowing what
it is like to be a woman.

Now all of this affects everything. When you
meet a young woman at church, and you are chatting with her, and wondering if you should ask her
out, all of these things that I am talking about are
running in the background. They are running in the

background in your mind and they are running in the background in her mind. And remember—they are running in the background differently.

If he is showing romantic interest in her, then one of two things is going on. He is either trying to figure out how to get into bed with her dishonorably, or he is trying to figure out how to do it honorably. Those are your options. Because she knows that something like that is in the cards, and because she is the one who could get pregnant, she is wanting to know what kind of man he is—the dishonorable or the honorable one. He is focused on how attractive she is, and she is focused on how reliable he is.

This is the point where critics will start yelling, as though I just said that a woman doesn't care about how attractive the man is. No, she absolutely cares about that also. But not the same way.

The woman getting pregnant is a huge factor in all of this, and one of the things that our abortion culture has wanted to do is to erase that as a factor—in order to put women on the same footing as the men. Birth control and abortion were intended to erase the clear and obvious difference I am insisting on recognizing.

But legal abortion does not really do anything of the kind—she is the one who gets the abortion and has to deal with the aftermath. A man can be the father of an aborted child, and never even find out, in this life at any rate. He will find out at the day of judgment, which will be bad. But still different.

I said earlier that the sexual differences between men and women are creational differences, marred by sin. But to say that they are creational differences is the same thing as saying that God recognizes them as real differences. When men and women sin with those differences, God doesn't approve of it in either case (because it is sin), but He does recognize the sins as being different sins.

We can see the difference easily out in the world of unbelievers. A man who has been with a hundred women is considered by them as a "player," while a woman who has been with a hundred men is considered the "club slut." From a biblical perspective, neither one is virtuous, obviously, but their sins are different.

So we cannot overlook such obvious differences. A man in that position could be the father of one hundred children. A woman could not be the mother of one hundred children. And this is because the roles of father and mother are completely different roles. Biology matters, and the world's propaganda machine notwithstanding, biology is not optional.

And one of the things that is assigned to us in the creation order is that when it comes to the consequences of the sexual act, women are betting with far more money than the men are. This is because they are the ones who get pregnant. Am I belaboring the obvious? It is because we live in crazy times and the obvious needs some belaboring.

When we are forced to recognize such differences (which we have to, because they are so glaring), we try to defend the egalitarian narrative by attributing the whole thing to society's "double standards."

The creation order itself is not egalitarian. Women are far more vulnerable to sexual consequences than men are. In response to this, one of the things that societies have done is to place additional safeguards around the women. This can be despised as establishing "double standards," and it is certainly true that this protection for the women has been abused in a way that defends a double standard—where women are expected to stay pure, and the men are expected to sow their wild oats.

So I need to be very clear here. It is not a double standard to say that the sexual sins of men and women are obviously different. It is a double standard to say that the sins of the men are not sins. If you count on the boys sowing their wild oats, while at the same time keeping your daughters buttoned up tight, that is the kind of double standard that Scripture condemns. It is a sin to wink at the sin of the boys, and prohibit the girls from sinning: "I will not punish your daughters when they commit whoredom, nor your spouses when they commit adultery. For themselves are not separated with whores, and they sacrifice with harlots: therefore the people that doth not understand shall fall" (Hosea 4:14).

And recall that time when Judah was going to have his daughter-in-law executed for "playing the harlot," as evidenced by her pregnancy, when he was in fact the father of the child. So Scripture recognizes the sinfulness of both sexes in sexual sin, and identifies it as sin. But this reality does not require us to pretend that the dislocations caused by these sins are the same. If a married man has a one-night stand with some other woman, the consequences for his marriage are severe. If a married woman has a one-night stand with some other man, and conceives a child, the consequences are more severe.

The fact that we have judges in our society that require men to pay child support for a child begotten by another man demonstrates how intent we are on trying to erase the differences between the sexes. It cannot work.

So it is not a double standard to recognize that men and women sin differently, and with different consequences. The prodigal son returns home, having been with multiple harlots, and is received with celebration. If it had been the prodigal daughter, with a two-year-old bastard, whose father was still off in a far country, she too would have been received home with gladness. The forgiveness can be the same, but the situations are still completely different, and the forgiveness in the latter circumstance would have to deal with far more.

When it comes to sexual matters, and your understanding of life between the sexes, you need to get every vestige of egalitarianism out of your system. You will be surprised at how it affects your outlook when you approach another woman. Not only will it affect your outlook, it will affect the reception you are likely to get. But more on all that in my next—this has been enough for one letter.

Your uncle,
Douglas

FOUR

CALVINISM AND GIRLS

Dear Dawson,

So this letter is going to be a discussion that combines your two favorite subjects—Calvinism and girls. Let me start by saying something you might think is problematic, and then see what I can do to work my way out of it.

If I were speaking to a group of young men, and I used the metaphor of a "sexual marketplace," the chances are pretty good that I would have a bunch of young men tracking along with me, and probably taking notes. "Man, I didn't know half this stuff!" If I were fool enough to do the same thing with a group of young women, the chances are outstanding that the indignation levels would rival a roomful of wet cats. Men are far more transactional on the subject, and women are far more relational.

To illustrate, suppose a young man moved into the area and joined your church, and he was of a marriageable age, and he proceeded to ask three girls out in the first month. The first two said, "No, thanks," the third went out with him once, and then said, "No, thanks." Word of his activities gets around. Suppose further that he asked a fourth girl out in the second month he was there, and they were engaged by the end of that month. The chances are pretty good that this young man will be tagged as someone simply on the hunt for "any willing female," and the levels of indignation, again, will be high. More on this in a minute.

(Now to clarify, men are far more transactional when it comes to sexual attractiveness. When it comes to long-term life together, their positions usually reverse. In that realm, women are far more practical and pragmatic, and the men are the romantics. But I will perhaps pursue that in another letter.)

In our generation, men generally have to hide how transactional they are with regard to looks, and this is because the feminine paradigm has become the orthodoxy for all. This is the result of the "victories" of feminism. Feminism has not altered the fact that men still rule, and still basically make the decisions. That is largely unaltered, and has even been expanding. After all, men are even taking over women's sports now, right? Men can still take charge over stuff, but it has to be in the name of the lie of empowering women. Feminism is in charge of the lie, but can't be in charge of reality. This is because reality is not optional, while lies about reality are optional, so long as they are believed.

So feminism has been successful in establishing the nature of the lies we must tell ourselves. The approved lies right now are the feminist lies. And one of the narratives that women like is a narrative that has taken deep root in our culture and has even persuaded a bunch of the men. This is the doctrine of "the One," and it is the underlying theme for any number of chick flicks. It is why that young man who knew he needed to get married, and who conducted himself accordingly, caused such indignation. If a guy asks four girls out in the space of a couple of months and marries the fourth, there is no way that he was in pursuit of "the One."

Now I am not saying that this fellow is wise. He might not be paying close enough attention to issues of godly character. He might not be doing his due diligence. He might actually be in pursuit of "any willing female." He might be rhetorically inept. There are all kinds of reasons why pastoral counsel for him might be necessary. But the reason he caused indignation among the ladies is that his theology of "the One" was clearly out of kilter. If he had swept into town, and the first girl he asked out had responded positively, that would have made all the girls go, "awwww," because that would have fit in with the doctrine of "the One." This is why the difference between "sweet" and "creepy" is often an underlying doctrinal one.

So do you want to get married? Well, the received wisdom says, somewhere out there must be "the One," and you just have to make sure to find that person. The hunt for that person then becomes semi-mystical, because we are trying to extract more information from our circumstances than we are meant to have. When you meet her, you will "just know." Well, no.

This lie has traction with Christians, in the form of initial plausibility, because we do believe in the sovereignty of God. We know that God has ordained all things for His glory and our good. We know that we are God's workmanship, created in Christ Jesus to do good works, which God prepared beforehand for us to do (Eph. 2:10). If God prepared good works in advance for us to do, then surely those good works would have to include the one you are to marry, the number of your kids, their respective sexes, the color of their hair, and so on. Your good works, prepared in advance for you to do, would have to include marrying this woman, not that one, and bringing up two daughters, not three sons, and so on. This is the Calvinism part. God does work all things after the counsel of His own will (Eph. 1:11). In this sense, God does know the name of the One for you. But that is God's department, not ours.

But that is not how the false doctrine of "the One" works as men and women pursue "that special relationship" in their romantic attachments. This doctrine is a counterfeit, and therefore obtains whatever plausibility it has from the reality that it is surreptitiously copying. The problem is that it arrogates to ourselves the prerogatives of the Almighty.

Now God does have a decretive will, and nothing happens outside of it, or against it, or contrary to it. This includes the good works that He has prepared for His people to do (Eph. 2:10), but it also includes the treachery of Judas (Acts 4:27-28). All this is to say that God has a purpose and plan for all things, one that encompasses and includes His sons and His slaves both, His beloved children and His tools and instruments equally. But we know that with regard to His children, His purposes and plans for us are for good and not ill: "For I know the thoughts that I think toward you, says the Lord, thoughts of peace and not of evil, to give you a future and a hope" (Jer. 29:11, NKJV).

Now many Christians have concluded from all of this that they are supposed to figure out what God's will is for them beforehand, and then to go and do it. They call this "getting the will of God," as though we were supposed to find out the will of God by carefully reading His published agenda for "the meeting" beforehand. And then we think we are supposed to follow that agenda to the letter, thereby staying in the will of God.

The only problem with this is that God doesn't publish His agenda beforehand. You are not going to find that Gabriel, that august messenger of God, has thrown a brick through your window with a note tied to it, saying, "Introduce yourself to Suzy Q. Lordschoice at church next week. She is the one. After a week of chatting her up, ask her out . . ." Nothing like that is going to happen, or, if it does, you need to check yourself into a hospital, the kind where they strap you into your chair.

So no. It is your task to live out the will of God for your life. You are to live it out, not figure it out. You are to do the will of God, and this is not the same thing as figuring out the will of God beforehand. Trying to figure out the will of God beforehand is only going to paralyze you and prevent you from doing the will of God. You don't pray to get the will of God before ordering off the menu, even though food poisoning is a possibility, depending on the entrée. You don't pray about changing lanes on the freeway, even though death and mayhem for all your passengers rides on it. This is why we trust the Lord and commit our ways to Him. Prying into His business is not the way to trust Him: "In all thy ways acknowledge him, and he shall direct thy paths" (Prov. 3:6).

We acknowledge, He directs. We have a tendency to want to reverse this. We want to direct, and we want God to acknowledge it somehow beforehand. But it doesn't work like that: "O Lord, I know that the way of man is not in himself: It is not in man that walketh to direct his steps" (Jer. 10:23).

The epistle of James rebukes the arrogance of those who think they have the future laid out in the palm of their hand:

> Go to now, ye that say, To day or to morrow we will go into such a city, and continue there a year, and buy and sell, and get gain: Whereas ye know not what shall be on the morrow. For what is your life? It is even a vapour, that appeareth for a little time, and then vanisheth away. For that ye ought to say, If the Lord will, we shall live, and do this, or that. (Jas. 4:13–15)

Our lives are a mist, a vapor. Our lives are like a little bit of fog, a yard long, that comes off the creek in the early morning hours, and when your car blows by it, it's gone. What we ought to say is "if the Lord will," we will do this or that. But we don't know. And we do not deal with the arrogance problem by claiming even more knowledge—"because we have decided it is the Lord's will, we will go into such a city, and make a pile of money."

I don't know if it is the Lord's will for me to be married tomorrow, and that is because I might die tonight. My wife might die tomorrow. Our lives are a mist: "The secret things belong unto the Lord our God: but those things which are revealed belong unto us and to our children for ever, that we may do all the words of this law" (Deut. 29:29).

So here is the bottom line. The secret things belong to God. The revealed things belong to us. If we have a clean desire to live in the will of God, we will demonstrate that through our eagerness to live according to what the Scriptures require of all Christians. If you want to live in the will of God, this means you must love your enemies (Matt. 5:44), forgive those who wrong you (Col. 3:13), read your Bible (Luke 4:4), stay away from porn (1 Thess. 4:3), and so on. These are the things revealed. Pursue these with a whole heart, and God will direct your steps. As far as we are concerned, the will of God is a moral issue, and who you marry is a wisdom issue. Your best path to the latter is an industrious pursuit of the former.

This means, not to put too fine a point on it, that you must marry a Christian (2 Cor. 6:14), a Christian who would not be disobeying God by marrying you (Luke 16:18), a Christian of sterling character (Prov. 31:30), a Christian whose personality gels well with yours (Amos 3:3), and a Christian whom you find sexually attractive (Prov. 5:19). These are all things revealed. The secret things are frankly none of our business.

Notice how the apostle Paul talks about a particular woman who is free to remarry after her husband has died. She must marry a Christian, he says, but after that, what? She is at liberty to marry whoever she wants: "The wife is bound by the law as long as her husband liveth; but if her husband be dead, she is at liberty to be married to whom she will; only in the Lord" (1 Cor. 7:39).

Imagine a devout Christian standing in the kitchen, trying to decide whether to have chocolate or vanilla ice cream, or the moose tracks. "Oh, Lord, thou knowest all things. Wouldst thou have me eat the chocolate or the vanilla? Or perhaps the moose tracks?" You are unlikely to get a reply, and if you did get a reply, it would be an impatient Gabriel telling you that you're the one that has to eat it.

We sometimes make the mistake of believing that we need access to the secret things of God to make a good decision, when the actual reason for our poor decisions is that we just skim over the things revealed, merely glancing at what God's Word actually requires of us: "For I say, through the grace given unto me, to every man that is among you, not to think of himself more highly than he ought to think; but to think soberly, according as God hath dealt to every man the measure of faith" (Rom. 12:3).

If I ask a young man if his pickup truck can pull her trailer, the natural inclination of masculine pride is to say yes. But is that judicious wisdom talking, or something else? I once was visiting with a young man about a particular young lady, and he laid out for me all the reasons why he thought she would be a real blessing to him. She was a lovely girl, and he was not wrong. But when I asked him for the reasons why he thought that he would be a blessing for her, you could tell that the thought struck him as a complete novelty. That is not a good place to be. Quite apart from the decrees of God, that is not the demeanor that God requires of us.

But put all of this together, and you will discover that this is why Augustine could say, "Love God and do as you please."

"Delight thyself also in the Lord; And he shall give thee the desires of thine heart" (Ps. 37:4).

"But seek ye first the kingdom of God, and his righteousness; and all these things shall be added unto you" (Matt. 6:33).

Your uncle,
Douglas

FIVE

NICE GUYS AND JERKS

Dear Dawson,

I think I have laid enough groundwork now. Let's go back and do some post-game analysis of your breakup with Jan. Now keep in mind that some of this might sting a little bit, but that is a whole lot better than the long-term chronic misery that results from not facing up to these sorts of things.

The point, of course, is not to rub your nose in the mistakes you made, but rather to head off and prevent similar mistakes in the formation of any new relationship. The first thing to recognize is the fact that you didn't see the breakup coming means that you probably still don't understand the causes of it. You were thinking of your position in the relationship as being stronger than it actually was (Rom. 12:3), and this means that you were looking at the wrong markers, the wrong indicators.

Some of what I am about to say Nancy and I both observed the few times we met with you guys, and some of it I am deducing from certain descriptions and phrases in your letters. That said, I think I am pretty confident about what happened. So here we go.

In your relationship, you were the quintessential nice guy and would turn yourself inside out to do whatever she wanted. And that is how you drove her off. Not only would you do whatever she wanted, it was starting to look as though you were willing to be whatever she wanted.

But a woman wants what she wants from two different places, two different realities—and both of those realities are formidable. First, she has certain desires that are built-in, part of her framework as a woman. She is created by God to respond to and follow her head, her husband. She is called by God to respect her husband, and she has a deep creational need to be with someone who is easy to look up to, easy to respect.

But a woman is also part of a fallen human race, and she also wants certain things the way all of us do. She, like everyone else, wants her own way. She has selfish desires, selfish moments, and things she wants to insist on—how you are going to spend an evening, what restaurant you are going to go to, whether or not you are going to go to that dance or not. Now if, when she is being selfish, she gets her way one hundred percent of the time, she knows that she is not being protected, not being led. Let's say you had a little spat, one that she was entirely responsible for, and at the end of it, in order to make peace, you were the one who apologized. That meant that you were trying to build your relationship with her on the foundation of lies—and she knew it. You were both lying, but she was more aware of it and didn't like it more than you didn't like it.

When you interacted with her in this way, you set her up for an internal conflict. There was a standing conflict between the way God made her and what her flesh wanted. As created by God, she wanted to look up to you and respect you. *She wanted to lose sometimes.* As fallen and selfish, she wanted what she wanted, like we all do. She wanted to win. More on this in a minute.

In a husband/wife relationship, the man is the appointed head. It would be tedious to cite all the verses, right? "For Adam was first formed, then Eve" (1 Tim. 2:13). "But I would have you know, that the head of every man is Christ; and the head of the woman is the man; and the head of Christ is God" (1 Cor. 11:3).

For a Christian woman to agree to marry a man—when she has a Bible and has read all those verses—is risky business. It is like she is being commanded to walk out on a frozen lake. If she has any sense at all, she will need to know how thick the ice is. So she might stomp on it. She might throw a cinder block on it.

And if you, steeped in those servant leader sermons you have heard at that church you go to, think something like, "If she likes throwing cinder blocks, then let her throw cinder blocks," there are many things you are doing there, but one of the central ones is that you are failing the test. She is not throwing cinder blocks for her health. She is throwing them because she is desperately hoping that she has found a guy where the cinder block doesn't go through the ice, and where he says something like, "Okay, you can stop that now."

Unfortunately, we live in a time when a significant portion of our evangelical leadership has come to believe that the phrase "man up" means that the men in every relationship have a responsibility to figure out what the women want, and then to go and do whatever it is. But that is actually the opposite of what it means to man up.

But remember that you also have a dual set of desires. You were created by God to be the head, which means that you have a deep creational need to provide for her and protect her. That is what you are by God's creation design. But you are also a sinner, and you also have your selfish desires. And one of those selfish desires is to have absolutely no conflict with your girl. Her selfish desire may lead her to demand something, your selfish desire leads you to acquiesce, and God's design for both of you is frustrated.

I should insert here the recognition that there are men whose selfish desires run in a different track than yours. You are a nice guy, and so your temptation has been to appease. There are other men out there who are royal jerks—demanding, censorious, critical, irascible, and all the rest of it. As you mentioned, the guy your ex is now dating is someone who runs along those lines.

But what should this tell you? It tells you that your ex was looking for something different than what she said she was looking for. This doesn't mean she was lying to you—the chances are excellent that she is as muddled on this question as you have been. But the fact remains that she told you many times that she was looking for sensitivity (which you, poor chump, tried to provide), when she was actually looking for authority—real leadership.

Now in dating a jerk, she is not getting the kind of authority that Scripture talks about. A biblical head is the authority in the relationship, but it is an authority that is direct, immediate, sacrificial, and true. Christian authority bleeds for others. So her current boyfriend is offering her a counterfeit, not the real thing. There will consequently be disillusionment for her at some point, if it hasn't hit already. But instead of you complaining about it, you should be taking a lesson to heart. That jerk is not being biblical, right? But his counterfeit authority seemed closer to meeting her creational needs than your counterfeit servant leadership was. When she went from you to him, she thought (at least in the moment) that it was an improvement. He was offering something that you weren't offering.

If Christ is functioning as the Lord of the relationship, both parties, the man and the woman, have their assigned domain. Each should respect the authority that the other has in that domain, and those responsibilities are laid down for us in Scripture. But the two are in a shared relationship as well, with shared territory, and there are many places where Scripture does not assign the responsibility. We know who is supposed to have the babies and nurture them (1 Tim. 5:14), and we know who is supposed to fight to protect the home (Neh. 4:14), but we don't know who is supposed to keep the checkbook. That has to be decided by the two of them. There are actually a host of decisions and responsibilities like this that have to be decided between the two of them.

Now, in such areas, it is crucial that there be significant areas where the wife gives way, where she does not get her way. And the reason should be obvious. If she always gets her way in those areas, it is going to become almost impossible for her to avoid the conclusion that she married a pencil-neck. Letting her have her way in all these areas is tantamount to consigning her to a life of frustration. Not only so, but the husband gets frustrated as well. So they then go in for marriage counseling, and they get this, their central and devastating mistake, endorsed by a pastor—whose own wife, incidentally, has cheated on him a couple of times.

So let me conclude with that example of the checkbook. Let us say that both want to keep the checkbook, and let us also stipulate that they are both decent at math. Both would do a good job. As they discuss it, it is important that the husband stay in fellowship the entire time, and not give way to any kind of frustration, annoyance, or anger. There will be other areas where the assignment goes to her, but here, he makes the decision that he will keep the checkbook. And in this decision, he must make it stick. He must win.

Now I am happy to put "win" in scare quotes here because a relationship is obviously not a competition. But in every relationship there will be moments where husband and wife must interact with one another as though they were adversaries. They are not, and if they are godly, they know that they are not. But there will be moments where that phrase *as though they were* must absolutely be remembered, and especially by the husband.

I mentioned earlier that a husband is assigned the responsibility of providing for his wife and family, and protecting his wife and family. Those are, on the practical level, his two central duties. They are

to be driven by love, obviously, that love being im-
itative of Christ's love for the Church. Christ loved
the Church, remember, but He did so through His
provision and protection.

And so if one of a man's central duties is to protect his wife, we now come to the bottom line.
Women usually have a much better instinct for this
than the men do. A woman knows that a man who
cannot stand up *to* her is going to have difficulty
standing up *for* her.

Your uncle,
Douglas

SIX

A MATTER OF RANK

Dear Dawson,

We are getting close to the current center of all the turmoil between the sexes. Now I use that word current advisedly. There has always been turmoil between the sexes, and the nature of that turmoil is handed down across generations in proverbs, customs, and lore. But something unusual has happened in our generation.

Up until very recently, men and women both understood the natural order of things. The man was the head of the home, and there you go. This was often violated in practice, in many different ways and for many different reasons, but everyone

more or less acknowledged the way things ought
to go. When it was practiced, it was honored, and
when it was not practiced, it was denied, hidden,
or named something else. This is because everyone
subscribed to the natural order. Everyone paid it lip
service, in other words.

It has been left for our time to abandon this
standard as a standard at all. Not only is it not
the standard anymore, it has now become a hate
crime to profess that you even think it should be
the standard.

The desire that a woman has to usurp the rule of
her husband is a desire that goes back to the third
chapter of Genesis. This is the source of the running
tension between the sexes. Finding and marrying a
godly woman is going to mitigate this tension for
you, but it will not erase it: "Unto the woman he
said, I will greatly multiply thy sorrow and thy conception; in sorrow thou shalt bring forth children;
and thy *desire* shall be to thy husband, and he shall
rule over thee" (Gen. 3:16, emphasis added).

Until this mortal life is over, this curse of mul-
tiplied sorrow is something that women have to
deal with, including saintly women. Childbirth involves travail, and this travail is shared by believing and unbelieving women both. So why should
the problems go away simply because we got to
the next clause?

The Lord tells the woman two things. First,
He says that her desire will be "to thy husband."

Secondly, He says that the husband will rule over her. We know that this is a desire to usurp the husband's authority for two reasons. The first is because of the context of the immediate past—this sin is what had brought about the Fall. Eve was beguiled and corrupted by the serpent, and took on herself a position that was not hers to assume. She was the one who took the initiative in the sin: "But I suffer not a woman to teach, nor to usurp authority over the man, but to be in silence. For Adam was first formed, then Eve. And Adam was not deceived, but the woman being deceived was in the transgression" (1 Tim. 2:12–14).

The second reason is the odd juxtaposition of the words *desire* and *rule*. This construction happens only one other time in the Bible, and it is found in the next chapter. In that place, God is warning Cain about the struggle he is about to go through: "If thou doest well, shalt thou not be accepted? and if thou doest not well, sin lieth at the door. And unto thee shall be his *desire*, and thou shalt *rule* over him" (Gen. 4:7, emphasis added).

Here the juxtaposition of *desire* and *rule* is a picture of a power struggle. Sin has a desire for Cain, but Cain must fight back and rule over it. In the event, Cain did not do this—sin had its way with him, sin fulfilled its desire. Cain did not rule over his sin the way he ought to have.

But husbands will rule over their wives. The woman wants to usurp the authority of the man, and he reacts, sometimes unkindly, and rules over her. It is a fallen world, and this is a distortion of what authority and submission would have looked like in an unfallen world. Nevertheless, this is how it is now, and it is this way because God has ordained it this way: "For the man is not of the woman; but the woman of the man. Neither was the man created for the woman; but the woman for the man" (1 Cor. 11:8–9).

In an earlier letter, I mentioned that women are torn between two impulses—what they are by virtue of creation and what they are as a result of the Fall. In the order of creation, the woman is a man's helper and companion, suitable for him (Gen. 2:18). She is his crown (Prov. 12:4). She is the glory of the man (1 Cor. 11:7). Her price is above rubies (Prov. 31:10).

But that is not the only order she lives under. In the order of sin, she is a *rival*. Not only a rival, but a constantly frustrated rival. Her recurring desire will be to usurp the authority of her husband, but in the main her attempts at usurpation will come to nothing, and he will rule over her. Patriarchy can be godly or ungodly, but it cannot be erased. If you spend enough energy, money and time jamming feminism down everyone's throats, the end result will be a bunch of dudes carrying off all the women's track and field trophies. Patriarchy wins again, and in this case it is a demented patriarchy. Feminism apparently doesn't mind being ruled by biological males, just so long as they are godless lunatics.

Now if an individual woman is a godly woman, dedicated to cultivating the submissive demeanor that the New Testament consistently requires of women (Eph. 5:22; Col. 3:18; Tit. 2:4-5; 1 Pet. 3:1-2), she will in large part rule over her own spirit by the grace of God. *That means that she can give her husband the very real gift of not having to live in a constant rodeo.* But this does not mean that she can be submissive to her husband without a second thought. No, this is every woman's challenge—whether she is in a good marriage, a bad marriage, or an in-between marriage.

And this brings us down to the pinch point. In every relationship between a man and a woman, including the godly ones, there will be *adversarial moments.* Now when you begin a new relationship, this reality is going to arise at some point, probably very early on. And when it arises, and it comes out that you are interacting with her *as though she were* an adversary, this is almost certain to hurt her feelings. She will say, perhaps plaintively, "I thought we were friends, lovers, not *adversaries.*"

You will tell her, if you have your wits about you, that you are indeed *not* adversaries. But you will add that there are moments when clarity of mind requires that two people who love each other dearly act *as though* they were adversaries. I said this in my last letter, and it is crucial that you remember it. When you are in this position, you are about to "pull rank," and so that brings up the whole question of rank.

In the Navy, a lieutenant outranks an ensign. That is simple enough. In my metaphor, everyone who believes this belongs to the patriarchy, the one that everybody keeps wanting to dispense with. Now everyone who believes this knows that when it comes to other qualities, it is quite possible for the ensign to be the lieutenant's superior—in intelligence, looks, personality, table manners, the lot. But, nevertheless, at the end of the day, the lieutenant outranks the ensign.

In a similar way, the husband outranks the wife. The egalitarian believes that this is an outrage and that this is the patriarchy that he desires to smash. At this point you might ask about complementarianism. Isn't that a third alternative? No. Complementarianism is simply an invertebrate form of the patriarchy, and feminists hate it just as much as they do the patriarchy. But because it is invertebrate, they want to squish it instead of smash it. In many marginal cases, a complementarian is an egalitarian who is still stuck with some Bible verses that have not yet been digested and are still important to the donor base somehow.

Now in a well-ordered biblical relationship, the practical authority structure functions in accord with the formal rank. "Wives, submit yourselves unto your own husbands, as unto the Lord" (Eph. 5:22). When a wife does this, what is happening in real time is the same thing as what Scripture outlines on the flow chart. Everything is rightly ordered.

But the disparities of ambition, talent, charisma, and sin can cause severe dislocations in a husband/ wife relationship. C.S. Lewis points to this dynamic in his essay on the inner ring, in the place where he quotes Tolstoy's *War and Peace*.

> Boris now clearly understood—what he had already guessed—that side by side with the system of discipline and subordination which were laid down in the Army Regulations, there existed a different and a more real system—the system which compelled a tightly laced general with a purple face to wait respectfully for his turn while a mere captain like Prince Andrey chatted with a mere second lieutenant like Boris. Boris decided at once that he would be guided not by the official system but by this other unwritten system.
> (Tolstoy, *War and Peace*)[1]

In every relationship, one person generally needs the other person *more*, and the one who needs the other person *less* is in control of the relationship. That is what happened to you in your breakup with your ex. You needed the relationship to work out more than she needed it to work out, and consequently, she was the one in charge, the one who made the decision. She was in control.

---

1. Cited in C.S. Lewis, "The Inner Ring," in *The Weight of Glory* (1949; New York: Macmillan, 1980), 93.

I have no doubt that there were certain episodes early on in your relationship where she tested you and found out that she was in fact in control. In the order of sin, there were times when she liked it like that, because we all like getting our way, but in the order of creation, she did not like it at all. And because she did not not like it at all, she came to discover at the end of the day that she did not respect you. And you were in the unenviable position of losing her respect *precisely because* you were doing what she demanded.

One last thing, and I will be done, at least for this letter. The Scriptures require two things of us that are relevant to all of these issues. One is the Bible's teaching on the permanence of marriage. That is important to everyone who believes the Bible. That is a significant player in this, because it is one that is absolutely worked by egalitarian women who pretend to be evangelical. Once the marriage has occurred, provided there is no flagrant adultery, that's it. This is why it is so important to emphasize that Scripture also requires wives—in multiple places no less—to not be insubordinate. This is because all Christian wives, in all Christian marriages, occupy a subordinate rank. And it is always bad for a subordinate to be insubordinate.

And if a woman's first instinct upon reading something like this is stumble over the word subordinate and to rush in to say something like, "But in Christ there is neither Jew nor Greek, slave or free, ensign or lieutenant . . ." your response should be to say, "That is quite correct, and entirely true, and also not what we were talking about." And your second response, internally, not out loud, should be to cross her off your list of prospects. You would both be miserable together. Believe me.

This is why it is essential that you look for a woman who loves the Word of God straight, no chaser. She needs to love the way God ordered the world, she needs to love the respective ranks appointed for husband and wife in the creation order, she needs to love the Scripture's description of these things, and she needs to respect and love you.

You must avoid, like the proverbial plague, any woman who cherry-picks her way through the Bible. If she has a high view of the permanence of marriage, and a low view of her responsibility to be submissive in that marriage, then the former promises to become your cage, and the latter will be the sound of her throwing away the key.

You should want to be with a scriptural sweetheart, and not with some egalitarian porcupine. This should not be difficult to understand.

Your uncle,
Douglas

SEVEN

THE NATURAL USE OF THE WOMAN

Dear Dawson,

Up to this point, I have perhaps said a number of unusual things, and in our day controversial things, but we are still just assembling pieces on the work-bench. We are now approaching the point where we will begin the assembly. I am talking about con-structing a biblical view of how a man and woman ought to enter into the marriage covenant. Once you have this clear in your mind, you will then be in a position to seek out a woman who has it clear in *her* mind. Or, failing that, if it is not clear in her mind because of the prevailing fog we all live in, you seek out a woman who is absolutely submissive to the Scriptures and is willing to learn what the Scriptures require of Christian women.

I am going to be using two analogies. The first will be the one I have already alluded to, that of assembling a complicated piece of machinery on a workbench. The second will have to do with novels—one written by a man for men, and the other written by a woman for women.

Let us start with the assembly metaphor. You no doubt have had the experience of putting something together, in a way that made sense to you, and then having the disconcerting experience of finding a piece left over. The unique shape of the piece declared to you the fact that you clearly left something out. It was nothing so simple as an extra screw, or an Allen wrench that was just there for the assembly. The piece was clearly meant to go inside the thing you just assembled, and now you know that your gizmo, whatever it is, does not have that piece, and it was probably an essential piece. And so you know that piece was intended to play a role. And its configuration clearly means that it will be useless unless it goes into its assigned spot.

Now suppose that you lived in a time when egalitarianism had almost reached its apotheosis. "Equality for all" was within reach, and that supreme moment was just around the corner. As a consequence, your workbench was surrounded by observers and critics and media pundits who were telling you that "all parts are equal." And because of the unique delusion that egalitarianism provides, what they meant by this was that "all parts are the same."

In the old order, you would have taken the whole thing apart again in order to discover your mistake, in order to find out where that part was supposed to fit. Your mission would have been to discover the unique role that it had to play in the irreducibly complex contraption you were working on. After all, you wanted the thing to *work*.

But in this weird new order of ours, wanting something to "work" is a clear vestige of white supremacy. And while some people (who don't get out much) might say that I am clearly letting my satiric bent get away from me, and that no one would ever say that wanting something "to work" was "white supremacy," I am afraid that we are actually way past that point. People are saying this kind of thing all the time, and we say it about profoundly important things. We say it, for example, about marriage.

We have people running our country who can't tell the difference between male and female, or between thieves and customers, or between sane citizens and the mentally ill homeless. This is not a side issue—major cities are rapidly becoming uninhabitable because they have a ruling class that believes that a functioning society is the hallmark of oppression. So you do not just have the challenging task of finding a good and virtuous wife. You must find her while living in a madhouse.

In the grip of egalitarianism, we want no *assigned* roles for anybody. The part that everyone gets to play is the part that they have chosen for themselves. You can be whatever you want to be. We do not want any authoritative assembly instructions coming at us from outside. That would be dictatorial, authoritarian, fascist. So each part must identify itself, in line with its own hopes, dreams, aspirations.

In the old order, in the Christian order, there are sex roles and sex rules. These roles are assigned by the one who designed the whole thing, and the fundamental sex rule is that we must respect the authority of the one who designed it all. It is He that has made us, and not we ourselves. It follows that He knows where everything goes, and where everyone should go.

This applies to the basic facts of biology—God says to the woman, "You are the woman, and so you shall have the babies." This also applies in areas that some consider less obvious—you are the man, and so when there is a loud noise downstairs in the middle of the night, you are the one who must go check. I say "less obvious," but we have to remember that it is only less obvious to us now because of the unrelenting dint of propaganda that we have been subjected to.

The glib and sophomoric response to this wants to ignore the fact that God designed everything about us, whether inside and out. So when I say that the one with the womb should make the babies, the response comes back that I do not apply this consistently. Why don't I say, for example, that the ones with *hands* should make the sandwiches? A fuller answer will have to wait for my second analogy, the one about the novels, but for the present I will just say that a woman's inner psychology is as uniquely configured as her womb is. Godly women want to feed their men. Godly women are designed to make the sandwiches. This is not an absolute law, like the one about making babies, and there are times when a man fends for himself and makes quite a decent sandwich. But in the general scheme of things, the apostle Paul wants the women to make the sandwiches. In Titus 2:5, Paul is saying that the older women should be teaching the younger women to be *oikourgos*—busy at home, keepers at home. That includes the sandwiches. And no, if a man and his wife go out on a lunch date, and their sandwiches are made in the back by some minimum-wage male, nobody is sinning.

If you doubt what I am saying about the unrelenting propaganda, try this experiment. Among your circle of friends, most of whom are evangelical Christians, try to make conversation this coming week in a way that will cause one of your friends to complain that you seem to be "stereotyping." It will not be hard. Say that women like cross-stitch more than men do, or that men are taller than women, or that women like baking pies for their men. And the conversations that will follow will be very predictable. Your common sense generalization will be considered "answered" because somebody has a aunt who is 6′2″, or a sister who hates making pies.

Because men and women are so naturally distinct, the task of the egalitarians has been to file down the uniqueness of their respective shapes so that they can assemble "families" according to whatever worldview whim or fashion takes them at the moment. So instead of thinking about heterosexual civilization as a complex Swiss watch, our generation—in the grip of this lunatic dogma, in pursuit of the brave, new family—want men and women to be Lego pieces that have had the male pieces filed off and the female pieces filled in. Everybody is now a little plastic block, and any piece can go anywhere. The only thing that distinguishes any block is now the color, and they are working on that.

The goal is nothing so simple as, "Let the homosexuals be homosexuals." That was just a preliminary step. No, the ultimate goal is for everyone to be metrosexual and androgynous. You have seen the periodic online outrage, have you not, where some tranny dude is complaining about the bigoted men who don't want to take him out? Make no mistake—this sexual-cargo cult is serious, and they have their own perverted version of the great commission. Just as Christ requires obedience from all nations, so these people are driving toward androgynous submission from all. The two worldviews are not reconcilable.

But notice something. In this brave new order, not only can any piece go anywhere, it is also the case that any piece is *entirely dispensable.* In the old order, your eccentric uncle had a place that only he could occupy. In the new order, a block is a block is a block. When someone makes up their own identity, the end result is an absolute loss of individuality. Have you never thought of walking up to someone with Halloween hair and saying, "What an *outrageous* idea. However did you think of it?" And the contrary is also true. When we receive our assigned station from the hand of God, and accept the fact that He configured us to occupy just such a station, the end result is true individuality, *sui generis.* There is nobody like your Uncle Wyatt. This is because the one who loses his life for Christ's sake will find it (Matt. 10:39).

We have been cowed into accepting all their absurdities because certain words or expressions have been designated as "offensive," and so even Christians have been badgered into abandoning them lest we seem insensitive. We have all been chased out of living useful lives because nobody ever wants to "feel used." But why not? What's wrong with being used? It is the great sin of homosexual men that they abandon the natural use of the woman. Is it not? "And likewise also the men, leaving the natural use of the woman, burned in their lust one toward another . . ." (Rom. 1:27).

When we have a just complaint that someone "has used" someone else, the problem is always with what they left out, and not with the use itself. All of us use one another all the time, and there is nothing wrong with it. This is what it means to live in family, or in community. The problem is not with using people, which is inescapable, but rather the problem arises when we use them in a reductionistic way. The problem comes when you use someone while forgetting who and what they are.

Suppose you are at a picnic late in the afternoon, and someone comes over to ask you a question. When you turn to talk to him, you find the sun is shining straight into your eyes, and so you lean back in your chair so that the guy standing next to your questioner blocks the sun. All of a sudden you can see everybody clearly. Are you using that fellow as a shade-maker? Of course. Quite obviously so. But are you using him as just a mere sun-blocker? We hope not. If he were to enter the conversation with his own question, would you say, "I don't think you are supposed to talk. You're just the umbrella"?

Now lust is reductionist in just that way. As Lewis pointed out, when a lustful man says that he wants a woman, that is actually the last thing he wants.[2]

2. C.S. Lewis, *The Four Loves* (New York: Harcourt Brace Jovanovich, 1960), 134–35.

What he actually wants is a particular sensation for which a woman is (currently) the necessary apparatus. A man who really wants a woman is a man who also wants a lawn to mow, bills to pay, curtain rods to hang, a van to buy, car seats to install, meals to share, and—let us not forget to include this—lots of good times in bed. He should want everything on that list and quite a bit more.

But nothing on that list is just that. As an old Puritan once put it, first a man must choose his love, and then he must love his choice. And loving your choice means the glad assumption of sacrificial responsibility for her, which is why there is no inconsistency between a man using his wife to help guard against immorality (1 Cor. 7:2), and a man laying down his life for her sake (Eph. 5:25). The same man can do both, and, making necessary adjustments, the same woman can be both. She can accept the propriety of her being used, and she should also accept the propriety of him being willing to die for her.

All that said, will there be times when a wife is tempted to think that her husband is taking her body for granted? Yes, of course, and there will be times when he probably is. But this is a fallen world, and there will probably also be times when he, up on top of a telephone pole in twenty-eight degree weather, thinks that she is taking his body for granted. Look. Things are tough all over. In a godly marriage, a man and a woman should use and be used, gladly, responsibly, sacrificially, and lovingly. That's the whole point.

So I will close with my illustration from novels—the kind written by men for men, and the kind written by women for women. I will get to that in a minute, but need to set it up first. The point of this illustration is to demonstrate how deep this creational orientation goes. God oriented men to women differently than He oriented women to men. Men and women do not think about their relationship in the same way. "Neither was the man created for the woman; but the woman for the man" (1 Cor. 11:9).

This is not an example of Pauline misogyny, but rather a description of the deep structure of the world. The man was created for the garden, and the woman was created for the gardener. He has a task in the world, which is to exercise dominion in the world. God saw that he was going to need help with this, and so He created a helper (Gen. 2:18). He created a "helper fit for him" (ESV), a "helper suitable for him" (NASB), a "helper comparable to him" (NKJV).

He was created for the mission. She was created to help the missionary.

Is Paul the only one who thinks this? No, we can gather up additional testimony from Jane Austen, Louis L'Amour, Homer, and Danielle Steel. It can be great literature (Homer, Austen), or it can be reading for the lake-cabin getaway (L'Amour, Steel). In the novel written by a man for men, the mission is central. They must find the gold, or win the war, or get the cattle back, or otherwise deal with the guns of Navarone. The plot is driven by that mission. When a women enters the book, she being a plucky rancher's daughter, what is her role? Well, she helps get the cattle back, and so on. In the novel written by a woman for women, the relationship is central. The relationship is the backbone of the plot. First they like each other, and then they don't like each other, or somebody else doesn't like them liking each other, and then they like each other again, fade to black.

In short, everyone thinks this. Everyone knows it. Men don't think about women the way women think about men. They aren't supposed to. It is just that we live in a generation when we have decided to rebel against this knowledge, and we are consequently seeking to live in a way that is "against nature" (Rom. 1:26). Part of our general sexual downgrade has been the result of women, even Christian women, thinking that men have a responsibility to be oriented to the relationship the same way the women are. This is false, not to mention pernicious. The results of this mistake are predictable enough and have been quite disastrous.

Your uncle,
Douglas

EIGHT

LACK OF COMMUNICATION IS KEY

Dear Dawson,

I am glad you have met a girl, at church no less, and it is good to hear that you have decided to ask her out. I have no doubt that I will have to explain this one a bit more, but if you ask her out, and if she says yes, always remember that lack of communication is key.

Let's say you go out to dinner, and discover along the way that you two can talk easily, naturally. You are a warm-hearted and expressive guy. What could go wrong? The temptation you will face is that of someone who has been nurtured on the propaganda of this present darkness, and that temptation will be to share, as opposed to making conversation.

If you don't watch your step, you are going to share, and she is going to share, and then you both share a little more, and then it gets tangled up a little bit, and first thing you know, the two of you are besties. A little bit later you are going to be trying desperately to figure out how you became her girlfriend. You don't want to be her girlfriend. But congratulations, you are now stuck in the friend zone, and she won't let you out of the friend zone because she is an evangelical Christian, and lesbianism holds no attractions for her.

So what is the difference between sharing and making conversation? If you sit down with her, and you start telling her all about your hopes, dreams, and aspirations, along with the fact that your long term goal is to be a screenwriter, you are sharing. You are unloading the truck. You have ramped the intimacy levels of your conversation way up to eleven. You are leaving her guessing about absolutely nothing. You have become a spiller of guts.

The danger in telling you this is that you might think I am encouraging you to play head games with her instead, trying to act like an international man of mystery. But I am not trying to get you to manipulate or lie. Rather, I am encouraging you to cultivate good manners and not to worry about the consequences of having good manners. The consequences will be good.

The reason you asked her out was because you thought she was attractive, and you would like to get to know her, and you are hoping that you make a good impression on her as well. Now if I told you not to pick your teeth with the salad fork at dinner, would you respond by saying that you want to be "authentic," and that you want her to get to know "the real you"? No, you would not, and if you did do something like that she wouldn't be getting to know the real you in any case.

There is absolutely nothing wrong with wanting to make a good impression on a girl you are taking out. All I am telling you is that part of making a good impression includes not acting like an emotional needy bucket. Some guys act that way because they are emotional needy buckets, and they do what they do naturally. But other men—and I put you in this category—act this way because you have been taught poorly.

The prevailing beta male culture of evangelical Christianity has taught you that you must overcome your natural male reticence about such things, and that you must cultivate openness and transparency and vulnerability. And if you are enough of a chump to believe all of this, you will find yourself in a truly baffling place. That is because girls do like this kind of thing, in that it is not unpleasant for them to be around it, but they are not attracted to it sexually.

If you follow the instructions you have been given in line with these broader cultural assumptions, you will find yourself friends with a girl who is not interested in you "in that way." Or, if you manage to get far enough into it that she is in fact in a relationship with you, the whole thing is going to be vaguely dissatisfying to her. This is what happened to you in your previous relationship. And this will be a grand mystery to her as well, because the women are being lied to as well as the men.

So, ride the brake. Lack of communication is key. Don't be like Hezekiah—don't show the Babylonians everything.

I distinguished this gusher kind of sharing from the entirely different approach of making conversation. So what are the characteristics of that?

This is the same advice that is regularly given to writers. They are constantly exhorted to "show, don't tell." There is no way to keep your dinner conversation on that first date from being a time of self-disclosure. Her interactions with you will tell her many things about you. But if you approach it wisely they will tell her these things obliquely, and they will leave her with the sense that there is much that you are holding back. And that is good. Lack of communication is key.

Ask questions. Ask her about her background growing up. Mention an article you read, and ask her what she thinks of the point the author was making. Ask her what she thinks of what the Supreme Court just did. Find out what her favorite novel is, and don't volunteer what your favorite novel is. Talk about the menu. Mention the time you brought your parents to this restaurant. And fight the temptation of thinking that this is all "small talk." Better to have a full man talk about small things in the world around him than to have a vacuous man unload absolutely everything he has, and arrange it pleadingly on the table in front of her.

Do not, under any circumstances, try to make her feel sorry for you. This is not because you won't get it. You probably will get it. Women do have a natural bent toward sympathy. They are good at extending sympathy to those in need of it. But they are not attracted to it. I have no doubt that your ex-girlfriend really did feel sorry for you in the very moment she was breaking up with you. But feeling sorry for you is not going to pay the bills.

So an interesting man is an interested man. But he is going to be interested in the world, in theology, in the woman he is with, and so on. He is going to be interested in where the salt and pepper shakers on their table were manufactured. He is not interested in spilling out or spelling out his emotional resume in front of her.

God has made the sexes in such a way as that when men are being men and women are being women, there is a vast territory where they do not understand each other at all. There is nothing wrong with this. And when men become convinced that this is a bug instead of a feature and seek to converse and interact and respond in such a way as to mirror exactly what the woman is thinking, this will be an incredible frustration for both of them. Moreover, if they have bought into the egalitarian lie, they will be mystified by the frustration. They won't know where it is coming from. The truth is that the source of their frustration is coming from the Pit.

Your uncle,
Douglas

NINE

THE VALUE OF GENDER STEREOTYPES

Dear Dawson,

By this point you have probably noticed that I have been engaging in what is now called "gender stereotyping." Perhaps you were brought up by such polite parents that you were able to look over it, acting as though nothing untoward had been happening at all.

What I would like to do in this letter is defend that practice, and perhaps even to explain it some. I touched on this in an earlier letter, but as your future marital happiness depends on it, indulge me for a few minutes while I defend the value of gender stereotypes.

The way our speech gestapo have fought against this practice is simple enough. Rather than provide an argument why such generalizations are to be avoided, they have resorted to the simple expedient of simply "being really offended" whenever it happens. In other words, if you talk this way, then you will be guaranteed to have negative experiences with the people around you. And since no one likes having those kinds of negative experiences, they start to police their own behavior. They start to self-censor. This is not because anyone has taken them through the steps of any kind of argument, but rather because they don't want to set anybody off or make a scene.

As I was writing this to you, a friend of mine said something sensible about women on Twitter, and that set off a Twitter-swarm. Looking for reasoned discourse in these swarms is like being attacked by thousands of mutant hornets, and wasting your time trying to identify the most diplomatic hornet among them so that you might have some constructive interaction. But these guys don't want to reason with you—their most developed argument runs along the lines of, "Shut up, you moron."

So the reluctance that so many have to make generalizations is probably the strongest evidence we have that the foundational assumptions of egalitarianism have taken deep root in our culture.

Even those who are not persuaded of these assumptions have agreed to be policed in line with them—which means that over time they are in fact being persuaded by them. This is how the egalitarianism of twenty years ago is the complimentarianism of today.

Let me first demonstrate the legitimacy of generalizing, and then go on to press it into the corners. Suppose that, in some public place like Twitter, someone uses their account to post something like this: "I'm generalizing of course, but men are taller than women." What can be said to this, besides, "Shut up, you moron?"

What does that "I'm generalizing of course" actually mean? It means that this person is saying something like, "For the most part, men are taller than women." Take the average man, and take the average woman, and the chances are pretty good that the man is the taller one. Take the height of one hundred random men, and the height of one hundred random women, average those respective sets of heights, and the average height of the male group will be taller than the female group.

This is simply the first stage of my argument, but I must hurry because there is probably a warrant out for my arrest already.

The phrases "I'm generalizing" and "for the most part" mean that the speaker himself knows that there are exceptions to his statement. He himself is 5'11" and his sister is 6'1". He knows that. This is why he said for the most part. The generalization, taken as a generalization, is true.

But we have been trained to think of stereotyping as the foundational enemy of justice. The thought is that because false stereotypes have been used in the past by bigoted individuals, it has become therefore necessary to ban all accurate stereotypes as a means of fighting bigotry. And yes, I said accurate stereotypes. Men are taller than women.

If you are debating this issue with someone in evangelical circles, that person might retreat to a position that says that stereotyping only becomes hurtful if you are saying something critical about a person—which being tall or short isn't.

But a critical generalization can be accurate also: "One of them, a prophet of their own, said, 'Cretans are always liars, evil beasts, lazy gluttons.' This testimony is true. Therefore rebuke them sharply, that they may be sound in the faith" (Tit. 1:12–13, NKJV).

Notice that Paul generalizes about Cretans, and the generalization is sharply critical. He plainly knows it to be a generalization because he grants an exception at the front end—a prophet of their own. He's not a liar, because Paul says his testimony is true. In addition, Paul instructs Titus to teach the Cretans in such a way as to make his observation increasingly inaccurate, as they grow to be more and more sound in the faith. This is a perfectly reasonable and pastoral way to think.

Now critical generalizations can be made about the two sexes as well. When the apostles say something like, "Now you men, don't do this . . ." or "You women, make sure not to . . ." what they are doing is generalizing by implication. When Paul tells men not to be harsh with their wives (Col. 3:19), he is generalizing in his assumption that men are more likely to be tempted with the sin of harshness.

And when he tells Timothy to place a hedge against the younger widows growing wanton (1 Tim. 5:11), he is generalizing and saying something about what ecclesiastical welfare checks might do to a young widow: "And besides they learn to be idle, wandering about from house to house, and not only idle but also gossips and busybodies, saying things which they ought not" (1 Tim. 5:13, NKJV).

That was a long buildup, wasn't it? What I am saying is that men and women are very, very different, and that the world is very, very sinful, and so their respective temptations and sins are going to be very different.

Now one of the temptations that men and women both share is the temptation of wanting the other sex to deal with the characteristic sins of their sex, while carefully leaving the characteristic sins of their own sex alone. The woman wants the man to sandpaper off the rough edges of his masculinity and quietly assumes that the standard of appropriate smoothness is set by her femininity. Now he does need to have that happen, and he actually needs a belt sander in certain places, but the standard for this is Scripture—not the woman's sensibilities. And the reverse is also true. He wants her to be more open and enthusiastic about sex, let us say, and he quietly assumes that his desires are the normal standard for what that ought to be. But again, the standard is Scripture, and not his desires.

Because we sin downhill, because we don't examine our assumptions as closely as we ought to, we grant the doctrine of human sinfulness when it comes to the other, and we quietly assume that our basic framework is what the Scriptures commend. But this is frequently not the case.

Scripture knows what the man is like and also knows what the woman is like. Scripture tells us that the relationship of a husband to his wife is hierarchical. Scripture tells the man to provide, protect, and love. Scripture tells the woman to honor, help, and submit. Now because obedience is the great opener of eyes, if a couple resolve to live this way, they are going to grow in their understanding. They are going to grow in their understanding of God, the world, their spouse, and themselves.

This means they are going to learn the value of gender stereotypes. They will be able to do this because obedience to the Word of God is in the process of turning them into sensible people. You know, normals.

Sensible people know that gender stereotypes did not force men and women into certain patterns

THE VALUE OF GENDER STEREOTYPES

of behavior. Gender stereotypes are not some strait-jacket to which we all must conform, however our free spirit within might protest. No, gender stereotypes are the wisdom of centuries, our reasonable reaction to the obvious differences between men and women, which, if honored and followed, provide the safest path to genuine happiness. A statement like this is easy for a feminist to rage against, and she might claim that my approach has been a cause of untold misery in the world.

But I would then ask why she, the liberated one, is so miserable, and why the conservative, traditional women I know are so happy and contented with their assigned station. And I will not be slow in providing the answer—such conservative women have been left free to be women. They have not been badgered into aspiring to things they never really wanted in the first place.

So then, we have seen that in this relativistic age such sentiments verge on criminality. If that is the case, then the remainder of this paragraph will be something of a crime spree. Men are taller than women, as established. Men are less emotional than women. Women are better at nurturing than men are. Men are more analytic in their thinking and women more intuitive. Men are more task-oriented, and women are more relationship-oriented. Men want to be respected, and women want to be loved. Men want to lead, and women want to submit and follow. Men are more interested in

sex than women are. Women are more communi-
cative, and men more taciturn. Women don't want
to follow a weak man, but they do want to follow a
strong man. Men have more upper body strength
than women do. Men are better at opening pickle
jars than women are. You get the drift.

And if you read through a series of statements
like that, and find objections, exceptions, and
counterexamples crowding into your mind, relax.
These are generalizations, after all. I have seen
plenty of exceptions myself, and could provide you
with loads of examples. Harry is garrulous, and Sally
is taciturn. Great. Let the exceptions be exceptions.
Your tall sister doesn't refute the generalization.

I said earlier than your future marital happiness
depends on making your peace with this overall
reality. The differences between men and wom-
en are the foundational creational reality. Gender
stereotypes are a cultural response to those creational differences. Sex roles in marriage, in turn,
are based on those gender stereotypes. And when
you have accepted those traditional sex roles going into marriage, it is like asking her to dance, and
you both go out onto the floor in order to waltz together. But without such agreed upon roles, you go
out there ready to polka, and she goes out ready
to tango. Lots of opportunity for marital misery. In
the end you wind up stepping on her feet on purpose, and she winds up kicking your shins on purpose. Not a pretty sight.

Let me finish with this. With all this said, you don't want to find a girl who is simply submissive to you. That happens sometimes to alpha males, and then they get burned when a stronger alpha shows up. If submission to a strong male is the only thing going on, you will frequently have a lot of bad consequences. So you don't want a woman who simply submits to you.

What you are searching for—and this girl you are dating sounds like she might be the one—is a woman who is submissive to God Himself, to His holy Scriptures, and then to the way that God made the world, and then last, as a consequence of all the preceding, to you.

Your uncle,
Douglas

TEN

WHAT WOMEN WANT AND WHAT THEY SAY THEY WANT

Dear Dawson,

I am glad your friend Lauren has agreed to go out with you again. Making it past the third date is a milestone. But you are still getting to know her, and she is getting to know you, and so you are both still navigating what can be a pretty treacherous path. Her dad is not a Christian and is uninterested in any of that courtship jazz, and so you will have to be the responsible one in all of this.

So here is the challenge. While are getting to know her, you are also growing in your sanctification. That means that you should be wanting to become the kind of person that the kind of person you would want to marry would want to marry. Shall I say that again, perhaps another way? You want to marry a godly, conscientious, and attractive Christian woman. Suppose you met one. Suppose that Lauren is that woman. What kind of person does *she* want to marry? Apply the golden rule. She too wants to marry a godly, conscientious, and attractive Christian man. When you meet the person you want, why would that person want you?

Now I know you love the Lord and His Word. You are a godly young man, and you really are conscientious in your walk with Him. So the black box in all of this, the mystery to be solved, is what goes into that word *attractive*. What makes a man attractive to women? You want to be becoming *that* while at the same time determining that she is the kind of woman you are interested in. And if she is that, then would she be interested in you? Complicated, right?

But certain aspects of this question are not mysterious. You take showers. You don't dress like you ran through a clearance rack at Goodwill. You stand up straight, and when you do, you are taller than she is. You have decent table manners. You are not ugly. If you took a survey of 100 people, they would all say you were "that nice-looking kid." So then, you have passed the pre-qualifying round. *But that is all you have done.*

So what is the mysterious part?

I am getting to that, but something else needs to be noted first. My topic down below is going to be addressing what women want as contrasted with what they say they want. But women, being members of the human race, are divided into two categories—regenerate and unregenerate. There are women who are walking with God and who honor His Word, and then there are women who refuse to walk with God and who refuse to honor His Word. Men are divided into the same two categories as well.

Because men and women have different natures, this means that their respective obedience or disobedience is going to be working on and with different materials. So you are navigating a sexual world that has four fundamental classes in it, not two. You have to interact with obedient women, disobedient women, obedient men, and disobedient men. The lay of the land can get pretty confusing because the obedient and disobedient from each sex share certain things in common, and they are wildly divergent in other areas. You need to know which is which.

This setup has created an opportunity for beta pastors to get in there and muddy the waters. They can say, for example, that obedient women want a man who is a "servant leader." But what they mean by this is a man who leads by serving, instead of what they ought to be pointing to, which is the more biblical pattern of serving by leading.

A godly and obedient Christian woman is going
to want a man who is capable of standing up to her.
This is because she is evaluating the strength of his
backbone. If he cannot stand up *to* her, then she
knows, instinctively, that he won't be able to stand
up *for* her. She knows this in her bones. She wants a
masculine guy, one she can look up to and respect.
That is the creational norm. That is how God made
the world. If God tells Christian women to respect
their husbands, and He does (Eph. 5:33), then an
intelligent Christian woman is going to want a
man who does not make that respect an arduous
or difficult task.

But things can get confusing, because the
chances are good that if she grew up in evangelical circles, the sexual catechism she learned might
be full of references to "marrying your best friend,"
"servant leadership," and "the most potent aphro-
disiac is when a man vacuums and does the dish-
es." In short, she may have learned all the beta-
bromides, and simply think that this is what the
Scriptures teach. But it is not. It is simply what a
conspiracy of effeminate MDivs have been teaching. At the same time, she really does want to live
the way God wants her to live. So it is your job to
mess with the categories.

The confusion created by this kind of scenario
is, I believe, what tripped up your ex-girlfriend. If
she had a basic need for masculine assertiveness,
and was not getting that from you, she could easily

be tempted by an ungodly form of masculine assertiveness in the person of the jerk she wound up with. If someone is in a desert, dying of thirst, and they come across a pond that has posted signs about possible toxic waste contaminating the water, depending on how thirsty they are, they could easily be tempted, despite the warning signs.

And here is the difference between what a woman wants and what she says she wants. In the final weeks of your relationship, she explicitly told you that what she wanted from you was more sympathy, more sensitivity and more understanding. So you busied yourself with ginning up more sympathy, more sensitivity, and more understanding, all to no avail. So then she breaks up with you, and goes on to team up with a guy with half the sympathy, a quarter of the sensitivity, and no understanding. And there you are, scratching your head.

But she was not deliberately lying to you. She had been lied to, just as you have been lied to. The lies start higher up in the teaching hierarchy. But whatever the cause, there was a decided gap between what she said she wanted and what she actually wanted.

You are going to face the same issues with Lauren. *Believe me. Trust me.* At some point in the very near future, she is going to test you. By this I do not mean that she will consciously think something like, "We have had our fourth date, so it is time for me to test Dawson." The chances are pretty good that she will be as unaware of the formal test as you would otherwise be. But if you listen to your uncle, you will not be unaware of it. If you listen to your uncle, you will be prepared.

And her testing you is not nefarious. It is a prudent thing to do. I alluded to this in an earlier letter. If you want her to walk across the frozen lake of your character, she has every right to know if the ice is thicker than a quarter of an inch.

I am going to walk you through a scenario here, and then state what I think that mysterious *kappa* element is. And that should do us for this round.

You should already know if she has a violent dislike of any particular food, and if you don't, you should check. She'll say something like, "No, I like all kinds." Then you should say, "Great, I'll make reservations for somewhere nice." While you are pulling in to the parking lot of that nice Chinese place, she will say something like, "come to think of it," she really would prefer Mexican. *This is your test. This is the moment.* You need to say—without the slightest trace of irritation—that you would be happy to do Mexican next time, but that your reservations are for here. This tells her two things. First, it tells her that you are not a pushover, and it also tells her that there will be a "next time." And you hop out of the car, and open her door for her.

I should mention in passing here that I know of a number of married men who, because they failed at this point, can only stand up to their wives by getting into sin. They get angry, or sullen, or go silent, or they flop in some other way. That is the worst. And the way they got themselves into that mess is by listening to the devil, abdicating themselves into a bad jam corner in the first place, and then they ask the devil to get them out of it. But you can't sin your way out of a situation that you sinned your way into. If you sin your way into a bad situation by abdication, then surliness and bad grace won't get you out.

So cheerful Chinese it is then. You will be tempted to think that you don't care whether or not you have Mexican or Chinese. What counts is spending time with her. Of course you don't care. She doesn't care either. What she actually cares about (whether consciously or not) is finding a guy who isn't pliable. The issue isn't the food. Of course she wants a guy who is *amiable*, but that is not the same thing as pliable. So don't be a pliable goober.

And this brings us to the mysterious element I have been alluding to. What makes a man attractive to a woman is the same thing that makes him attractive to women generally. You are not meeting one another as the only two people on a desert island. This is all happening in a social setting. There are other girls. There are other guys. People are watching. And when Lauren discovers that you have the horse power to lead her, she realizes that you would also have the horse power to lead other women too. And she begins to suspect that the others have probably noticed that fact. You have become, to use the parlance, "a catch."

This is a reality that believers and unbelievers respond to differently. In the world of pagans, there are flirtation games, attempts to provoke jealousies, overt comparisons, and such like, and I am not talking about playing any of those sexual head games.

What I am saying is simpler than that. You have a circle of acquaintances and friends. It would be lawful for you to ask any number of girls out. You should comport yourself in such a way that the average woman in your circle would be interested in accepting the offer if you were to ask her out. And as a Christian, you don't do this by flirting with all of them. Rather, you do it by standing up straight, walking into a room with confidence, tackling hard things, working with your hands, knowing your own mind, and getting Lauren to try the almond chicken.

Your uncle,
Douglas

ELEVEN

THE ZONE OF VULNERABILITY

Dear Dawson,

The next thing I would like to cover with you has to do with the broader issue of authority, hierarchy and submission, and how these Christian concepts are in a death match with every form of egalitarianism.

There are two things we have to understand about how authority works in all of this. The first is that in order to be healthy, a relationship between a man and woman has to be under authority, and that authority must originate outside the world. Another way of saying this is that in a godly marriage, there are three parties involved, not two.

There is the man, obviously, and there is the woman, equally obviously, but underneath, over, and surrounding them on all sides, is the authority of the living God.

The living God is in the picture, and He is in the picture, of necessity, authoritatively. There is a genuine three-way relationship, but that relationship involves the Creator, and two creatures. The Creator created the man and his wife, male and female He created them, in the image of God He created them (Gen. 1:27). The authority that exists within the marriage, that of the husband, does not arise from him. Rather it is delegated to him by the Creator of marriage, and God has given him very explicit instructions on how that authority must be used, and how it must not be abused.

This means that a marriage, a relationship between a man and a woman, along with the authority and submission involved, is an *artifact*. It is designed. It is intended to function in a certain way. It is not supposed to be conducted in ways that cause it to function poorly, and it is not supposed to be conducted in ways that keep it from functioning at all.

A Phillips-head screwdriver is designed to do certain things, like screw in Phillips-head screws. It is not designed for certain things which it might still be able to do, like stir the sugar into your coffee, or using two of them in lieu of chopsticks. Still less is it designed to serve as a soup spoon. It is not made for that.

When we look at certain modern forms of egalitarian approaches to marriage, we should just
shake our heads and say, "Male and female were not
made for that." A woman can be the breadwinner
for the home, and he can be a stay-at-home dad, for
example, and you can certainly prove to me that it
can be done. And I will respond by stirring the sugar into my coffee with a screwdriver. It can be done.

If we try to play the relativist, wondering aloud
how it might be possible to figure out what this design for marriage might be, I have good news for
everyone. The Creator, the one who did all this for
us, *wrote a book*. The artifact comes with a manual.
There are training videos that accompany the soft-
ware. He tells us what to do. This is the authority
over marriage that comes from outside the world.

So when God tells us what to do, He does so
from a position of authority. The manufacturer is
telling you how to treat the equipment that you got
from him. He is the authority. But we live in a fallen
world, and there is a wide range of aptitude among
men and among women. This range of aptitude—
resulting from natural gifts, upbringing, education,
personal obedience, and so on—means that some
men are going to have an easier time of it, and some
women are going to have an easier time of it.

Some men will struggle being masculine. It is
a bigger challenge for them than it is for others.
Some women will struggle being feminine. It is a
bigger challenge for them. Because we live in an

egalitarian age, these unfortunate people are told to camp out right where they are and to feel aggrieved when they can't attract a man or a woman from that default position. Instead of picking up the genuine challenge of pursuing biblical masculinity or biblical femininity, they decide instead to complain about society's "stereotypes."

You are fortunate in that you have certain secondary external things working for you—you are tall, have a deep voice, a good baseball arm, and a nice beard. You look like a *guy*. But because you have been taught and trained by egalitarians, you no doubt flinched when you read that. So let me address that flinch first. The world of egalitarianism wants to flatten everything, and wants to do so at the expense of that which is higher. Egalitarianism is just a fancy word for *envy*. They don't want to make things less disparate by lifting up the less fortunate, but rather by taking down the more fortunate.

You are blessed with these sorts of visible things, and the envious want to shout them down or take them away. You are told that you should not care about such things at all, and a young woman who is considering you should absolutely not care. In this strange new world, you are allowed to be attracted to someone, but under no circumstances should you ever say why. If you say why, then someone will get angry with you. "So you're saying that you wouldn't ask a girl out if she had brown hair?" You have no doubt seen this response pressed to ludicrous extremes when trannies complain, feeling seriously aggrieved, that guys won't ask them out.

Every form of egalitarianism wants to be catered to. They want to promise everyone a living wage, affordable housing, guaranteed minimum income, free chocolate milk, and the sex partner of their choice. But of course, if everyone has the right to demand such things, then somebody else has the obligation to supply such things.

So instead of women working to become the kind of women that genuinely masculine men would be attracted to, they rather believe the duplicitous lie that they should "want a man who loves me the way I am." There is a truth in the middle of that lie, incidentally, which is what makes it so hazardous.

But we also have to take all this and factor in time, and stages of a relationship.

This is what I mean. In a courtship relationship between a Christian man and a Christian woman, you do not yet have that assigned part that Scripture assigns to the husband. She does not yet have the part that Scripture assigns to the wife. This is because you are not yet husband and wife.

When you are unmarried and you are pursuing a girl, you are trying out for a part. You do not have the part and should not act like you have the part. You are trying out for the part. It is a rehearsal, a playacting. In the scenario of the restaurant choice I mentioned in my last letter, you were playing with counters, and not with real money. What both of

you are learning is whether or not you know how
to play the game, but you shouldn't ever be playing
for real money unless there is a covenant in place.
There shouldn't be real money involved until there
is a ring on her finger.

In this, you know the role you are supposed to
play, were you to marry. She knows the role she is
supposed to play, were you to marry. But you are not
married. You have no right to act as though you have
that role already, and no right to expect her to act like
the wife already. This is one of many reasons why
you must act like a Christian gentleman throughout,
particularly when it comes to sexual behavior.

If you get the role, then you will be the head. If
you get the role, then you will be the final earthly
authority in the home. But before you get that role,
she is the authority. You already told me that her
dad is out of the picture, so who makes the decision? Well, she does. You are trying out for the role
of the lead, and she is trying out for the role of the
female leader. But she is also the director, running
the audition.

Let's say that there were ten guys pursuing her.
They would all be trying out for the part, and the
part would be that of becoming her authoritative
head. But who makes the authoritative decision
that selects one of the ten? She does. She is running
the audition: "The wife is bound by the law as long
as her husband liveth; but if her husband be dead,

she is at liberty to be married to whom she will; only in the Lord" (1 Cor. 7:39).

Notice that key phrase—to whom she wills. She makes the decision, and then she submits to the one that she decided on. She places the crown on his head, and then honors him as the one who wears the crown.

The reason I used the phrase "trying out for the part" is that it is perilously easy for a man and woman to settle into a kind of semi-permanent relationship. They are going steady, or they are boyfriend/girlfriend, or something comparable, and this nondescript thing can go on for months or years.

When this happens, it will either get sexual or it won't. If it gets sexual, then they are guilty of fornication, and this means that if they break up, what they have is all the emotional damage of a divorce, but without the attorney's fees. If it doesn't get sexual, then this introduces additional funkiness into their relationship. A man and a woman together in a relationship are supposed to be sexual, and if over an extended period of time they are not, then they are learning some very bad habits and are very likely frustrating one another.

A dating relationship is fun, and therefore it is easy to settle down in it. But settling down in it is dangerous, really dangerous. Having a girl on your arm Saturday night is fun, but that doesn't mean you should do it. Hanging out at a restaurant with her is fun, but that doesn't mean you should do it. Kissing her is fun, but that doesn't mean you should do it.

Suppose we were to draw two parallel lines, up and down, and we put all the guys on the far left side of one of the lines, and we put all the girls on the far right of other line. With me? Between the two lines is what I call the zone of vulnerability. That is the zone that you can't get out of without getting hurt or damaged in some way. If she is in the zone and you break up, she gets hurt. If you are, then you do. Frequently it is a tangled mess where both do.

Now it is not a bad thing to live there—God intends for us to live there. But He wants us to live there in some secured fashion, tied off with a covenant. That is what marriage is. Without a covenantal commitment, you don't have any business wandering into the zone, and you certainly don't have any business luring her into the zone. If you make that mistake, then there you are in a long term relationship, surrounded with unspoken commitments, with nobody quite sure of where everything stands. That's the way it was with you and your ex, right? You thought you were in one place, and she thought you were in another.

Enough for now.

Your uncle,
Douglas

TWELVE

THE GOLDEN RULE, WITH ADJUSTMENTS

Dear Dawson,

If you are any kind of a Christian at all, you know about the Golden Rule. All kinds of people know about the Golden Rule, in fact, including many unbelievers. What many people do not know is that the Golden Rule is a rule that sometimes requires spiritually sensitive adjustments.

Here is the rule: "Therefore all things whatsoever ye would that men should do to you, do ye even so to them: for this is the law and the prophets" (Matt. 7:12).

The rule seems simple and straightforward, and so what do I mean by this dark reference to "sensitive adjustments"? The Golden Rule is one that operates *mutatis mutandis*, which means "after the necessary adjustments are made." In other words, the Golden Rule is a bad rule, Dawson, when you are shopping for birthday presents for your mom. You don't buy her what you would like her to buy you for your birthday. Simple, right?

Yes, simple enough. But there are layers, and depths, and swirling currents at the bottom of those depths. George Bernard Shaw put it this way: "Do not do unto others as you would that they should do unto you. Their tastes may not be the same."

This is not a rejection of the Golden Rule, despite surface appearances. It is actually an additional application of it. From the Confucian adage, negatively stated, "Do not do to others what you do not want done to yourself" (Confucius, *Analects*, 15:23), to the Christian version of the same thing, positively stated ("do unto others"), we see different applications of the same basic principle. With that in mind, if we then look at the Shavian example, we see the same thing—the same basic principle, applied while taking certain additional factors into account.

A husband shouldn't buy his wife a shotgun for Christmas with the idea that is what he would like to get. His wife should not buy him a very nice string of pearls because then she could then borrow them. These are areas where their differences would skew a wooden application of the Golden Rule and would wreck the Golden Rule if applied.

But if either of them broke a leg, they would both want to have it set and treated by a competent doctor in the same basic way. This is because their broken bones are similar enough to be treated in the same way.

And so why am I giving you all this Golden Rule stuff?

Men and women are really different, from the tops of their heads to the soles of their feet, and this includes all the emotional and spiritual elements along with it. But because we all have been barraged with egalitarian dogma nonstop, we have half-persuaded ourselves that we really are all the same "inside." With this dogma to sustain us, we then go out into the world, where men and women act in very different ways. How do we account for those differences? Well, we tend to assume that the person who is acting differently must be perverse in some way. There is something wrong with him. This is the basis for so much that is simply masculine being dismissed as "toxic masculinity."

But it is not all "differences." What this means is that clunky handlings of the Golden Rule can result in a great deal of hilarity. A man and a woman can sit next to each other in a geometry class, and they can both learn that parallel lines don't ever meet. Not only so, but they can drill each other on that fact in the study group they both attend. They can

both learn the same thing, and they can both answer that question correctly on the test. This sort
of illustrative fact is something that we might want
to consider as God's little joke on us, designed to
make us think that we both think and reason and
respond in the same ways. The only problem is that
it is not true. We are still very very different.

We are similar enough that we can communi-
cate. We are different enough that such communication often goes astray. Sinful reactions to this
reality, from both men and women, tends to compound the miscommunication. And then bad doctrine about all of this (egalitarianism) results in everybody being mystified. And irritated.

What this means is that men must study wom-
en in order to learn what they need to know, and
women must study men in order to learn what they
need to know. We must do most of this work in our
life together with our spouse after we are married,
but young men would be well advised to get a head
start by studying their mother, their sisters, their
aunts, female classmates, and so on. All this is done
in a diligent effort to find out what the heck is going
on. If it makes you feel any better, women have to
study men too.

"Husbands, likewise, dwell with them *with understanding*, giving honor to the wife, as to the
weaker vessel, and as being heirs together of the
grace of life, that your prayers may not be hindered"
(1 Pet. 3:7, NKJV).

And the older women need to "train the young women to love their husbands and children" (Tit. 2:4, ESV).

If husbands need to dwell with their wives with understanding, they are going to have get that understanding somehow. If women are to be dedicated to loving their husbands, they will need to be trained by experienced women. Believe me, there are some very important things here to learn, and if you don't learn them, you won't know them.

Now all this is building up to something very important. This principle applied to the details of life together is always good for laughs at marriage conferences when you are speaking about the differences between men and women, and doing so to a mixed audience. Men and women are elbowing one another all across the auditorium. But I am not here talking about the fact that women are "more this" and men are "more that." That is necessary and helpful in its place, but there is something more foundational that must come first.

Given the fact that a man with characteristics abc is going into a relationship with a woman with characteristics xyz, it is necessary for him to have an a priori demeanor towards those characteristics xyz, and that demeanor has to be one of a settled sympathy. And if he finds a woman who has a settled determination to be sympathetic towards his characteristics abc, what is taking shape in that relationship is what people used to describe as a "match made in heaven."

When Paul tells husbands to love their wives as they love their own bodies, this is nothing less than an application of the Golden Rule to marriage (Eph. 5:28). Do as you would be done by. But remember the Shavian qualification. Do as you would be done by if you were a woman in her position.

Now questions might crowd into your mind. How on earth am I supposed to know that? The answer is that you must study. You must read. You must ask your dad questions. Talk with your sisters. And when you ask your sisters a question, and you get some answer that throws you into a state of nonplussedness, do not use the occasion to mock and sneer. Compliment your sister on her sage approach to life in general, and studiously take notes with a furrowed brow. This is stuff you need to know.

Now I used the word sympathy above, as distinct from the more trendy word empathy. Here, the man must sympathize with the woman, and he must do so intelligently, but he must not forsake his basic orientation as he does so. Empathy has the connotation of a complete relinquishment of your own perspective, in order to complete identify with the other. This is why empathy demands that we make no judgments at all, while sympathy can maintain an outside perspective that is frequently a helpful corrective.

Earlier I said, "Do as you would be done by if you were a woman in her position." But if you were a woman in that position you would want a man step in to help—so you never stop being that man. But you should be a man who sympathizes with her. If a woman is drowning in a river of sorrow, empathy would mean you throw yourself in next to her so that she can drown together with you, her new girlfriend. But if you sympathize, your heart goes out to her, and you keep your foot on the bank to extend a hand or to throw a rope. You can identify with her without ceasing to identify with yourself. Your own interests and perspective do not evaporate—you love your neighbor as yourself, which together with loving God, is the law and the prophets.

It goes the other way also. A wise woman will sympathize with her man in his situations, despite the fact that she has no natural inclination that way herself.

Let me give you one test case, a very practical one, and then on to a final illustration. This is a generalization, but in a married relationship, the man is usually more interested in frequent sex than the woman is. For the sake of this illustration let us say that a husband would like sex to occur twice as frequently as she would like it. After the honeymoon, which distorted expectations for both of them, they eventually settle into a married routine, with him wanting more than she does. So how is this to be navigated?

My only point here has to do with the demeanor that each of them should have. That demeanor is that the woman needs to sympathize with (not resent) his desires. She married a man and everything that comes with that.

That demeanor means that he needs to sympathize with (not resent) her level of desire. He married a woman, and everything that comes with that. Part of the allure of being with a woman is found in the fact that her thinking about sex is different. When you find a sex partner who thinks just the same way, you are in a homosexual relationship—which of necessity is vacuous, monotonous, and sad. The flamboyance of gay men is not a natural ebullience, but is rather an attempt to shout down how dull it is.

So she thinks to herself, "Of course he wants more. He's a guy. Poor baby." And he thinks to himself, "The twins are still toddlers and are putting demands on her body all day long. And then I come home with bedroom eyes, the last of the toddlers . . ."

This is a Golden Rule relationship. It is characterized by sympathy and mutual forbearance. They meet in the middle.

This how harmony is supposed to work. A man sings his pitch, and it is a completely different note from what the woman sings. Sin is not when we act like men, or when the women act like women. Sin is when we sing our assigned note flat or sharp. And when the man and woman are each singing flat or sharp, or both, the results are horrendous. When they are completely different, but on pitch, the result is harmony.

So, as you are taking this girl out and are not married to her, you are not yet in a position to practice all this. So what basic demeanor should you be looking for in her? What can you look for now? And if I were advising her, I would ask the same thing. What should she be looking for in you? The answer to both questions is the same.

You should both be looking for the obvious capacity to sympathize with people who are not very much like you at all. Because, after all, that's just the kind of person you will marry, whoever it is.

Your uncle,
Douglas

THIRTEEN

TESTOSTERONE DOES STUFF

Dear Dawson,

We now come to what used to be quaintly called "the facts of life." But instead of dealing with what we used to have, which was embarrassed fathers talking over sexual matters with embarrassed sons, we are now living on the tail end of a generation or more of what we have called "sex ed." That unrelenting sex ed drive in our government schools has been a potent mixture of grooming and lies.

And leave it to the government. After a generation or more of government-sponsored sex ed, the end result is that nobody is quite sure what sex even is anymore.

It is the lies you have been told that I am chiefly concerned with in this letter. The central lie is that sexual differentiation is an outside-in matter, instead of an inside-out affair.

This is what I mean. The fact that people can seriously maintain that making a man a eunuch is the same thing as making a man a woman, and that they can do this while maintaining a straight face, maintaining their medical credentials, and maintaining their driver's license, is a plain indicator of how many flights of stairs we have fallen down.

A man is a man from the inside out. A woman is a woman from the inside out. The XX chromosomes are found in every cell of the body, as are the XY chromosomes on the other side of the aisle. The idea that a man can achieve "womanhood" by cutting off the male protuberance and putting on a dress is a howler for the ages. Try taking a steer to your nearest veterinarian and asking him why your cow can give no milk. Put him on a monthly retainer and ask him to research it for you.

And these XX and XY chromosomes are not just cellular signage down in the cell, like the words on old-fashioned restroom doors. These chromosomes are blueprints, sets of instructions, directives, decrees, and *ordinances*. And one of the things they dictate is that a body like yours is going to have about ten times the amount of testosterone sloshing around inside you than your future wife will have. The amount of testosterone in our bodies varies according to circumstance, but taking one thing with another, a man will have way more of it that a woman will have.

This will result in things like you not understanding her at all, and her not understanding you at all. But remember that this is a design feature. God made it this way for a purpose.

Now this testosterone does stuff. It is not what you would call an inert substance. Testosterone is rowdy, aggressive, combative, interested in women, along with a few other things that used to give your mother fits.

If a man full of testosterone is disobedient to the law of God, then that will make him toxic, true enough. But if a woman full of estrogen is disobedient to the law of God, then that can make her bitchy. That also is true enough. But it is the *disobedience* that does the damage, not the baseline starting point.

In an earlier letter I used the example of a man hitting his pitch, and a woman hitting her pitch, with the result being harmony. But if a man sings sharp then he is doing the blustering machismo thing. If he sings flat, then he is being an effeminate pajama boy. If a woman sings sharp she is a harridan, and if she sings flat she is a mousy little doormat. I will develop this more later on but we are living in a time when a man hitting his masculine pitch, just the way he ought to sing it, will be described as toxic. Our generation is not musical, and hates the harmony most of all.

In the meantime, if a man and a woman insist on singing sharp or flat, then we should pray that they find and marry one another, thus making only two people miserable instead of four.

If you get in an argument with testosterone or estrogen considered as such, you are complaining about gravity making you stick to the sidewalk. If you take up a quarrel with XX or XY chromosomes considered as such, then you are arguing with deep creation. If you get into a spat with beards and breasts, you are arguing with Jehovah God. Not the way of wisdom.

In fact, because I am feeling mischievous, let us call testosterone the Great Stereotyping Hormone. Testosterone is like a caricaturist, sitting at his drawing table down in the cellular basement, trying to figure out how to convey things like beard, brawny forearms, deep voice, upper body strength, and many other suchlike hurtful generalizations. Left to his own devices, the caricaturist will come up with someone like Gaston.

Now here is the thing—we live in a generation that wants to throw everything in a gender blender and come up with some kind of androgynous bi-pedal carbon unit. You can be anything you want to be, so long as it does not reflect the image of the Creator, male and female (Gen. 1:27). "Whatever turns you on . . . no, no, not that." If you tell them that traditional heterosexual normativity turns you on, they will denounce you for a perverted hater.

They would rather you be turned on by your sis than by your cis.

The sexual revolution, at the end of the day, turned out to be a war on sex itself—because sex itself is ineradicably binary. The revolutionaries wanted to overthrow the old sexual order, and thought they had it within them to come up with a new one. But all they could do with this intricate sexual clock we were given was to smash it, and then play with the pieces. When someone points out that they can't tell what time it is anymore, they reply that "telling time is a social construct."

The reason they wanted to do this is because testosterone is angular and unwieldy. In order to build their brave new world, they needed a population that was a lot more docile than the one God gave us. As Lewis has Filostrato say in *That Hideous Strength*, because they were after absolute control, they wanted to work with geldings and oxen instead of stallions and bulls. As that wicked man put it, "There will never be peace and order and discipline so long as there is sex."[3]

Now to my point. One of the principal tools they have used for the accomplishment of this has been the widespread acceptance of pornography. Porn is a lying cheat, a flatterer. Some layabout male living in his divorced mother's basement is told that he is the master of a thousand women—he has an entire

3. *That Hideous Strength* (1945; New York: Scribner, 1974), 170.

seraglio down there, the kind that Suleiman the Magnificent himself might have envied. The porn tells him that he is "so bwave, so hansum," which is kind of like him playing *Call of Duty* all night and coming up to breakfast in the morning expecting to be given the Medal of Honor.

Porn is enervating, emasculating. Porn and masturbation in tandem are a great engine of our modern plague of effeminacy in men. And this happens while the man concerned is being lied to—the porn makes him feel like he is running a surplus of testosterone. He is a sexual being, after all, and he has needs after all. He is so masculine that he needs an relief valve. So he thinks he is overflowing in all his excess masculinity when he is actually dampening it. Just as smoking pot makes you feel wise and insightful, so porn makes you feel like a dude. But it is an optical illusion. It is a lie. This generation has welcomed in pornography wholesale, and one of the observable results is that you are not the man your great grandfather was. Testosterone levels are dropping at a rate of about 1 percent annually.

I am not making a simplistic point here—that drop in testosterone levels does have multiple factors going into it. *But none of them are good.* Another one of the factors is the unrelenting propaganda campaign being conducted against the kind of masculinity that remains a standing threat to their entire project. True masculinity is attracted to risk, and standing up to despots is risky. And enervated males want the security of cradle-to-grave government health care.

So that caricaturist down in your DNA wants to do more than put a beard on you. He also wants you to conquer something, climb something, collide with something. What is it that makes two rams run straight at each other in an epic battle on that mountainside? Is it the patriarchy? Is it stereotypes they picked up in kindergarten? Or is it the testosterone?

And testosterone is a package deal. You cannot limit its effects to sexual interest and activities. With a lot of testosterone you do get a generation of men who are highly sexed. But you also get skyscrapers, football games, skydiving, and moon landings.

Civilization is a device that God has given us that is capable of harnessing this testosterone. Men are the dominant sex, and will always be dominant. The only question concerns whether that dominance will be constructive or destructive. If it is destructive, then it will be destructive and brittle machismo or it will be destructive and limp effeminacy—a wreck either way.

But if masculinity is to be constructive, then it must be assigned responsibility and honored for taking up that responsibility. If you do what our generation has done, which is to revile all men who take up such responsibility, then you will drive a number of them into destructive forms of masculinity, and drive the remaining responsible men into hiding.

These responsible men are the ones who keep the whole thing going, but "off-budget," if you will.

So if you outlaw constructive responsibility on the part of men, you should not be shocked or dismayed with the devastating results you get. Civilizations are built by men who have families to feed. Civilizations are maintained by men who care what happens to the children they beget.

Now I am saying nothing about your relationship to porn because I do not know, and I am not accusing you of anything. But you would have to be a block of wood not to be allured by the ubiquity of porn—because the lie involved is both sweet and dangerous. But please know they are lying to you about the sweetness and the danger both. Sexual uncleanness promises a really good time, but the end is not sweet at all. "How I hated instruction, and my heart despised reproof" (Prov. 5:12). And that is related to the danger I am describing, which is that of a massive cultural castration—the devastating results of which you can see all around you. Porn separates the fun from the fertility and as a long term consequence loses both the fun and the fertility.

There should be no shame in pursuing a woman because you know that you need a lawful sexual relationship. That is not all that is involved, but that *is* involved. At your stage of life, you should have this as your number one goal or priority. Find a woman of good character who loves the Lord, who is submissive to His Word, a woman you are attracted to. Then buy a ring, rent a church, and promise before God and the assembled witnesses that you will pay for all the orthodontic work for however many kids you have.

From your most recent description, your girl Lauren sounds to me like she is that one. So what are you waiting for? You are burning daylight, man. Don't you *want* to sleep with her?

And if you flinched at that comment because you think that Lauren would be miffed if she thought you might be thinking "that way" about all of this, remember that you have ten times the amount of testosterone that she does. Of *course* you are thinking about it differently. You don't expect her to think like you do. Why should she expect you to think like she does?

Your uncle,
Douglas

FOURTEEN

APOLOGIES THAT LIE

Dear Dawson,

I am glad things are going so well, and I am doubly glad that you have been given an opportunity to apply what we have been talking about in your relationship with Lauren, and you have seen it bear good fruit. Her reaction to all these things has been especially telling, and good. And to top it off, you now tell me that the ring is actually in your possession, just waiting for an opportune time.

So with all that said, we are getting near the end of what I would like to leave with you, but as we do so, I want to go back and develop something I touched on in an earlier letter. What I said earlier was this:

Let's say you had a little spat, one that she was entirely responsible for, and at the end of it, in order to make peace, you were the one who apologized. That meant that you were trying to build your relationship with her on the foundation of lies—and she knew it. You were both lying, but she was more aware of it, and didn't like it more than you didn't like it.

(An earlier letter)

What I want to talk about here is the importance of truth-telling in a relationship. But in order to do that intelligently, we also have to address the nature of truth-telling.

First, Christians are followers of the one who is the Truth (John 14:6). We should therefore be people who speak the truth. The Ten Commandment prohibit false witness (Exod. 20:16.) Colossians says that we are not to lie to one another, now that we have put off the old man along with his deeds (Col. 3:9). And the lake of fire is reserved for liars (Rev. 21:8).

We have talked about this before, and so I know that apparent exceptions might occur to you. When everyone else is oohing and aahing over someone's baby at church, you don't have to volunteer that it is the ugliest baby you have ever seen. Refusal to volunteer that is not dishonesty, but rather good manners. And if you point to the Hebrew midwives deceiving Pharaoh, you are leaving something very important out. You really don't want your relationship with Lauren to be like Moses and Pharaoh. Right?

When deception is justified in Scripture it is because there is a war on, or conditions that are tantamount to war. In situations where you want the opposite of warfare, where you want comity and peace, the commandment is strict—truth-telling is foundational. Do not bear false witness against your neighbor. Do not lie to one another (Lev. 19:11).

Many relationships that move into open enmity and then divorce do so because back when "things were better" they weren't really better at all. Lying in a relationship is corrosive, and it is the kind of corrosive that will destroy the relationship.

And so in practical terms that means you should never apologize to your wife unless God believes that you wronged her. If, according to the Scriptures, you were out of line in your behavior toward her, you must be eager to seek her forgiveness. If you wronged her, put it right. And under those circumstances, she should never have to ask for an apology: "And be ye kind one to another, tenderhearted, forgiving one another, even as God for Christ's sake hath forgiven you" (Eph. 4:32).

This should characterize your relationship, and the traffic should go both ways. When you are annoyed with her, and you express it, then you should put it right. When she is emotional toward you, unjustly, she should put it right. Tender-hearted, forgiving one another.

But there is a vast difference between this kind of forgiveness, offered and received as a means of restoring fellowship, and the kind of apologies that are (frequently) sought as a means of maintaining the upper hand. Apologies that are tools in the service of various kinds of power dynamics are an enormous threat to your marriage.

I once knew of a situation where a husband had a problem with porn, which we all know is no good. But the surprising thing was that when he started to address it and get the victory over that sin, it caused difficulties in his relationship with his wife. This was because his sin would put him in the doghouse, where his guilt told him he belonged. And it is not possible to lead spiritually from the doghouse, and that part of it the wife kind of liked. She was willing to lose a bishop to take a queen.

That is an example of real sin having this effect. But the same kind of power dynamic can happen with "sin" that is simply asserted by the wife, and "acknowledged" by the husband, whether or not there was any sin there. He acknowledges it simply and solely for the sake of ending the quarrel.

If he makes up after a quarrel by apologizing for "what I did," and she accepts it, and yet he could not tell you exactly what it was that he did, then he really is sinning against his wife, against his marriage, and against the spiritual integrity of his home. He is sinning against his wife by lying to her. Not only is he lying to her, he is lying to her about the condition of their relationship.

If he is saying, "I am really sorry, honey," and he is thinking to himself what a piece of work, the best way to describe this kind of thing is as the preliminary groundwork for the divorce. It is truly no good.

One last thing about all this. Many times this kind of thing gets jumbled up and confused because of the sin that comes into the quarrel later. Let's say that the wife starts a quarrel over a trifle, over something that he did or did not do that really should not have been a problem. Say that he didn't say happy anniversary when he first got up, but waited until he got out of the shower, when he thought she would be awake. Something like that. Something dumb and stupid.

Now let us say that after fifteen minutes of trying to explain himself, he gets to the point where he loses his temper. Now he really does have sin to confess. Now he really does have something to apologize for. And when he seeks forgiveness for that, his wife takes it as an apology for the whole shooting match and magnanimously forgives him. And he can't say anything about it because he is the one who lost his temper. He is acutely aware of the distinction between his earlier attempts to explain himself and his subsequent loss of control, but it is a distinction he is not in a position to make.

And this is one of the reasons why, whenever we have started something unfair, we frequently keep going with that issue until the other person loses their cool. This is because we can then assume that their subsequent sin has somehow provided a retroactive justification for us having started the whole thing in the first place. It isn't, but one of our private spiritual hobbies is the practice of kidding ourselves.

If this is a problem (and there will be temptations for it to become a problem), there is really only one way to deal with it. And that is to prepare yourself spiritually for an encounter with your wife (or soon-to-be fiancé), an encounter in which she thinks you were thoughtless, or insensitive, or too abrupt, or something in that neighborhood, and you do not believe so, and you work it through with her, all the way to the end, without losing your cool, and without apologizing.

Try it. Easy to describe, and very hard to do. Most men want peace and quiet in their homes more than anything, and sadly, many men are willing to lie in order to get it.

So if you do this right, you will experience two things. One is her respect. That is the first thing. That is the foremost thing. She wants to be married to someone who knows his own mind, and who can stand up to her. The second is the experience of your conscience deep inside you staring at your own behavior in utter disbelief and saying, "I hardly know you, man!"

Your uncle,
Douglas

FIFTEEN

DON'T MAKE YOUR WIFE A LESBIAN

Dear Dawson,

If you don't mind, I am going to repeat myself a bit. You can consider this letter as something of a summary of everything I have written to you over the last few months—with maybe some new stuff here or there.

It has become something of a custom in evangelical circles to use Father's Day as an occasion for kicking the men around. But in these sessions, the charge to "man up" has taken on a very specific meaning, and that meaning is that the men are supposed to find out what their wives really want, and then to do their level best to try to deliver that, nothing but that, and with no back chat.

The move was ingenious because it tells the men to do what the men really ought to be doing (acting like men), while at the same time filling that phrase up with effeminate content.

The standards for married life are given by God to the man and to the woman. They are not given by the woman to the man, and they are not given by the man to the woman. These standards, outlined for us by God in His Word, teach us to build on the foundation of the created order, while at the same time budgeting for the reality of sin.

There was an old saying, "It's a man's world," and the last generation or so has done its level best to flip that script, such that we must now say, "It's a woman's world." But actually it is neither—this is God's world. His standards make sense, and nothing else makes sense. If we listen to Him, we know that the foundational sexual order is good, as it was His idea, and that men sin in ways that disrupt that order, and that women sin in different ways to disrupt that order. Feminists and masculinists get into their arguments about which way should prevail, but that is like arguing whether it is better to fall off the right side or the left side of a horse.

One of the central ways that God's creative design in the formation of sex is denied is through a blind faith in a blind evolution. Evolution is a distortion of everything. It makes us assume that everything is haphazard and ad hoc, and that we can jury-rig things however we want. What this does is wreck our obligation to be grateful—and gratitude is essential to every happy marriage.

And why would sex have evolved anyway? Organisms prior to the "evolution" of sex had figured out a way to multiply without a partner, right? Isn't that a secure way of doing it? What evolutionary advantage was it to the first organism that decided to outsource this, making it dependent on the luck of finding a mate? And why did that mate happen to evolve the counterpart sexual organs that would even work? And what were the odds of these two freaks meeting and liking each other? Not a smart move.

So sex is an invented thing, an artifact. It is not the end result of a blind process—the result of time and chance, acting on matter. As a created thing, we see that it is involved in everything, it affects everything. If God fashioned this, when He was working with the dust of the ground, He was creating a man the entire time. And when He took Adam's rib to fashion the woman, He was creating a woman the entire time. This means that our sexual identities permeate every aspect of our interactions. We do what we do, all day long, as a man, or as a woman. Each of us has an assigned nature.

So God is the Creator God, overseeing all of this. Because we reject evolution, and affirm the foundational doctrine of creation, it follows that we must also affirm the doctrine of providence. God super-intends everything. But the secret things belong to God—and the things revealed belong to us and to our children (Deut. 29:29). This means that we must not try to wrest the control of providence out of God's hands. What I mean by this is that we shouldn't fall for the doctrine of "the One." This means that when you are "surveying the field," you shouldn't be thinking about how to figure out which one is "the will of God for you." He has a decretal will, but He is not going to tell you what it is. You should select a mate in line with "the things revealed." Does she fear the Lord? Does she revere His Word? Are you at-tracted to her? Does she look up to you?

But the fact that you found her, and like her, and she likes you, does not change the fact that there will still be power dynamics in your relationship. God has assigned you the role of serving as the head of the relationship, and she is going to want to test you, to see if you are up to that challenge. When she tests you, she (simultaneously) wants you to win, and she wants to win. If she wins, she will have gotten what she wants, but at the same time (at a deeper level) she will be disappointed in herself—but especially in you. If you are the head, and you are, then you need to demonstrate that you are capable of serving in that role.

We are souls and bodies together, and our souls have a spiritual nature that was designed to animate a physical body. We are more than animals—created

as we are in the image of God—but we are not less
than animals. The husband and wife have physical
needs that are the result of having physical bodies.
We have sexual needs. We have a need for compan-
ionship. We have a need for progeny. This means
that a man and his wife must learn how to (lovingly) use one another. The fact that we tend to recoil
from any use of that word use means that we have
not shaken off our Gnosticism completely yet. A
moment's reflection should reveal how necessary
this is. For a man to say that he refuses to "use" his
wife for anything means that he is actually saying
that he doesn't need her. That doesn't sound so attractive, does it?

In your relationship, you want to take care that
you prioritize giving over getting, obviously. But,
at the same time, it is not possible for a man to
give to his wife sexually unless he (physiological-
ly) wants to receive something also. He can't give
unless he is receiving, and something analogous is
going on with her.

You also want to give what the Scriptures tell you
your spouse needs, and not every little thing that
enters your head. There is such a thing as overshar-
ing, and so don't do it. One of the things you need
to give to your wife is your self-confidence. And if
you are running everything by her for her approval
first, that is not self-confidence. She needs a man
who wakes up in the morning knowing what he
thinks. She needs a man who keeps certain things

to himself. She also needs a man who talks to her, and so he has to figure what kind of conversation is a gift and what kind of conversation is him imitating a sucking chest wound.

God doesn't expect us to get to know our spouse starting from absolute scratch. He has given us a head start, and has done this through also giving us mothers, and sisters, and movies, and books, and . . . stereotypes. Stereotypes are simply generalizations that extend over multiple generations. Women tend to be this way, and men tend to be that way. Only an idiot would assume that this is an inviolable rule, like triangles needing to have three sides. So treat it for what it is . . . a head start. You have a lot to learn, and God has been kind to you by making women alike in many ways. Stereotypes are not bigotry, but rather are a way of navigating a very complicated world.

At the basic creation level, your woman wants exactly what you want, only from the opposite side. When you come together in that way, God is on both sides of the equation, and the result is great blessing. At the level of someone who struggles with sin, just like you, your woman wants exactly want you want, only from the opposite side—you both want your own way. In this sort of situation, the devil is on both sides of the equation, and the end result is a lot of unhappiness.

If you want your wife to make room for you and your masculinity, then show her how that is done—by making room for her and her femininity. It is certainly all right for you to be a man, right? But it should follow that it is more than all right for her not to be a man. And that means you should strive to be distinct notes, to use my earlier illustration, but with each of you hitting your pitch, and with a resultant harmony. You making space for each other is why the Golden Rule will be liberation for you both. You won't be giving the other what you would like to get. You are giving what you were designed by God to give.

The only way this can work is if the Holy Spirit is indwelling both of you. Your marriage needs to bound together by the God who alone can make it glorious.

You will be tempted to sin in your relationship, but the name of that sin is not testosterone. Initiative is good. A certain level of aggressiveness is good. Your desire for sex is good. All of that is the invention of God. You didn't think all that up, He did. Problems arise when you take those good things, and twist them around in ways to "suit yourself." When you do this, you wind up blunting the good things themselves. You think that testosterone demands masturbation, but masturbation is an enervating vice.

And to wrap it all up, remember that lying is a very poor foundation for a good marriage. Commit yourself to the Lord, and He will direct your paths. This means that you must reject the kind of apologies that seek to patch things up dishonestly. Apologies that lie are no good for both of you.

Take these things to heart. Put them into practice. If you do, then you will find yourselves happily married, as a man and a woman. You have not turned yourself into a girl friend which, if you succeeded, would make your wife a lesbian. Nobody wants that.

Your uncle,
Douglas